CAR
THE FATHER'S
FIRE

HOW 50+ERS WILL
HELP USHER IN
THE GREAT HARVEST

JOHN BONECK

CARRYING
THE FATHER'S
FIRE

*Carrying the Father's Fire: How 50+ers will
help usher in the Great Harvest*

© 2020 John Boneck, Tega Cay, SC. All rights reserved.

ISBN: 9781654641825

To contact the author: john.boneck@gmail.com

Unless otherwise indicated, Scripture quotations are taken
from the New King James Version. Copyright 1982 by

Thomas Nelson, Inc. Used by permission. All rights reserved.

Cover and Layout design by Kandi Evans

Dedication

To Sandy, the double blessing in my life.

Acknowledgements

The 50+ prophetic intercessor team members (Patti, Karen, Cathy, Linda, and Darlene) have met with me weekly for several years. I know they have protected me from my own choices. They have covered me and helped me to be more than I ever could have been without their spiritual guidance and insights.

Rick Joyner, the rest of the MorningStar Ministries team, and MorningStar Fellowship Church have allowed me to discover, practice, and implement the next thing the Father desires. I am truly blessed. And, thank you, Mary Jordan for reading and rereading the manuscript to catch the little things that make a big difference.

Table of Contents

Introduction

As I approached the end of the year, I sat in my orange leather chair in my home office, thinking about the coming year and my vision and goals for the future. I am not always strongly goal oriented, but my years in the business world helped me recognize the benefits of setting goals.

I started listing some spiritual goals for the coming year in my journal, wanting to be focused on what the Father was leading me to. I added some personal challenges in the goals that I believed would honor the Lord.

After I finished, I continued to think about my ideas for the future. Then the Holy Spirit interrupted my thoughts and started sharing the Father's plan. He instantly had my attention although He shared in a quiet way. He said,

The fire of God is coming! It will cleanse our minds, burning away past sins and failures from remembrance. It will change our vision and how we see around us. Holy heat will flow through people, and Godly glowing will be on individuals. Tongues of fire will return.

This will be a new day, a day of the Lord, the time of the Great Harvest. It will be like the Great Awakening from the past but will be unlike any we have heard about. It will be unique and different.

Suddenly, the spiritual goals I had already written for the coming year lost their luster. My goals were simply an extension of my Christian walk. The Father was talking about something greater.

I wasn't prepared for what He said. It had so many implications. What does that fire look like? What has to change in my Christian mind, in my thinking and living, about Father God and His will? What will we see that's different? What will we be doing? And, how should we respond?

To understand the fire of God, we first must know the God of fire. Part One of this book will connect us to the Father and connect Him to us in a personal way. We can't bring His fire if we are not intimately connected with Him. Part Two of this book reveals ways we get to carry His fire, making a profound difference around us as Godly fire starters.

A glorious blaze is about to happen on the earth, and we get to be part of it.

PART ONE: KNOWING OUR FATHER

Don't Mess With Fire

Our God shall come, and shall not keep silent;
A fire shall devour before Him,
And it shall be very tempestuous all around Him. (Ps 50:3)

O f all the images I could use to help describe our God and Father, fire is one of the most problematic.

When I was about 5 years old, my brother and a neighbor poured a little gas on the ground and set a match to it. The grass was quickly consumed in the blue and yellow flames. Not understanding the dangers of gas and flame, I picked up the coffee can that held the gas, held it over the fire, and poured it down.

I watched as the flames ran up the stream of gas. The next thing I knew both my hands were on fire. It didn't hurt at first, but then the pain began. I shook my hands. The fire remained. I ran from the backyard to the street and rubbed my two flaming hands in some dirt, putting the fire out.

But the damage was done.

I had to live with the pain. I couldn't tell my mother what had happened. I knew I would be punished. So for days I suffered silently. I watched as big blisters formed on the palms of my hands, still not letting on to anyone that I was hurting. I sat in the back seat of our Oldsmobile, staying in the car when the rest of the family went to visit some friends. I needed to be alone to be able to cry. The blisters were big.

After several more days the blisters finally began to burst and heal. Fortunately for me, mom and dad weren't the wiser.

Lesson learned: Don't play with fire.

Throughout history, mankind has had to relearn that lesson. Every year we hear about forest fires started by some careless camper or smoker. We know but we don't know, it seems.

It can also be true of any of us in encounters with our God who "is a consuming fire." Somehow we just don't believe the fire that heats our religious camp stoves might also burn down our religious forests if we are not careful.

After all, fire can be really good. It cooks our meals, making it possible to live healthy lives. It heats our homes in winter, supplying comfort and warmth. What could possibly be wrong with fire? It's even fun to play with. We light sparklers on July 4th and wave them in the evening air, creating pretty, colored patterns.

Yes, fire can be really good. And we'll talk about that in depth a little later because that's where I want to live. But first let's elaborate on the "severity" side of the "goodness and severity" of God that Romans 11:22 mentions.

The Israelites had ample opportunities to learn their lesson about fire, just as we do today.

Moses first meets God in a burning bush that isn't consumed. Who is this God who reveals Himself in fire? He calls to Moses from the bush and declares He is the God of Abraham, Isaac, and Jacob.

Moses can't even look at Him he is so afraid.

The God of fire continues, telling Moses He has seen the

oppression of the Israelites and is going to free them from the Egyptians. This fiery God is helpful, not harmful.

Moses starts learning something of the character of God. We must also learn more of His character in the move of the Father that's coming.

The Israelites don't seem to catch on as quickly as Moses does. Mostly, they don't understand Him. They see God perform a "seven wonders of the world" type of miracle display, freeing them from centuries of bondage. They cross the Red Sea on dry land, looking back on the Egyptians' bodies that wash up on shore after the waters close around the pursuing army. They receive pure water when they think they are about to die in the wilderness. They receive food every morning. Then, if that isn't enough, when they complain, the God of fire sends them quail to eat as meat.

Then comes Mount Sinai.

God instructs Moses to tell all the people that they will be God's "special treasure." They are to be "a kingdom of priests and a holy nation." (Ex 19:5-6) The God of fire who did all the wondrous acts also wants them as His preferred nation.

And their response is? Well, when a whole mountain quakes because God comes down in fire on the top of Sinai, you'd probably tremble just as they did, as Exodus 19:14-16 describes. Moses tells them, "God is showing you who He is so that you will remember and not sin." (Ex 20:20)

As a child attending our Pentecostal church in northern Wisconsin, I didn't actually tremble when hearing about God, but I knew He wasn't to be messed with. As a matter of fact, about all I knew about God is that He is to be feared.

One of my most vivid childhood Bible story memories is the story of Elijah and the priests of Baal. The priests keep trying to call the fire of their gods down to consume their sacrifices. I even had a 45 rpm record I listened to that told the story. When the fire of God comes down on Elijah's drenched offering and consumes it after the priests of Baal failed all day, the people cry out, "The Lord, He is God; the Lord, He is God." (I Kings 18:39) I knew this God of fire wasn't to be messed with. I think our church people may have viewed God the way the Israelites in the wilderness saw Him. He is fearful, and He has a lot of laws to obey, or else.

Today non-Christians and many Christians don't even think of a God of fire who interacts with us in a personal way. He doesn't strike us dead if we aren't perfect. So, no harm, no foul. However, thoughts about this God are about to change.

Back to Moses and the Israelites. God speaks to Moses, and Moses goes back to the people with some instructions God gave him on the mountain about feasts, about how they were to conduct themselves in their daily lives, and about Sabbaths. Moses tells them that God spoke him on the mountain and he is to give the people these instructions.

"And all the people answered with one voice and said, 'All the words which the Lord has said we will do.'" (Ex 24:3) This sounds a little like a foxhole conversion.

Moses returns to the mountain to receive more instructions. The children of Israel watch from a far-off distance. As they look, "The sight of the glory of the Lord was like a consuming fire on the top of the mountain in the eyes of the children of Israel." (Ex 24:17)

But, hey, God is there and so is Moses. We're here. What should we do? Moses spends 40 days on the mountain, getting more instructions, and the people make their own god, a golden calf, and worship it while he's away.

I would like to judge them, but how often do I have the Father's pleasure and favor in my life, and I somehow forget about it? I look at circumstances and try to figure out the best course, even making my own plans my idol instead of trusting the One who created me as part of His holy nation.

The issue is how we view God.

The children of Israel were terrified by this powerful God. Yet Exodus 33:11 says, "The Lord spoke to Moses face to face, as a man speaks to his friend." So, which is it? Are we to be terrified by this loud, on-fire God, hoping He doesn't punish or destroy us? Or, is He our friend, someone we actually have a relationship with? Or....is He both?

After all, our Father is coming again, and He is bringing His fire. He is going to start fires in people's lives around the world. I have already seen some of this.

Holy Father; Holy People

You shall be holy, for I the Lord your God am holy.
(Lev 19:2)

How do I have a kingdom relationship with this God of fire, trusting that He will not burn me up if I get too close or do something wrong?

Besides that, not only is He a God of fire, He is a holy God. He seems to be making it pretty hard for me to have a relationship with Him. If He doesn't burn me up, He'll probably judge me for not measuring up to His holiness.

Years ago, when my vocal chords were more flexible, I sang solos in church. One hymn I loved to sing was "Holy, Holy, Holy, Lord God Almighty." I sensed there was something special about God, our Creator, and was personally moved every time I sang it. I knew He was holy. I also knew He was not to be messed with. I didn't know, however, how to truly be holy as He is holy.

For decades I viewed Him with my Old Testament perceptions of someone who punishes those who are disobedient, as He did the Israelites. He even talks to Moses about destroying them all and starting over.

As we all know (because we've read the Old Testament), the Israelites fail many times to measure up. Holiness isn't easy to achieve, it seems. We can't achieve it on our own.

Growing up in church, I knew "Jesus loves me." He is my "personal Savior." I was taught God is a holy God, and we are holiness people—no dancing, no smoking, no using the word *darn*, and be careful about putting on too much make up. Being holy seemed to me to mean following a lot of commands and rules in order to please God. They weren't all bad rules. It's just that I had to keep track of them all.

Not only did we have to follow rules. We had to work to please him. Going to church three times a week and working hard were ways of living out our Godly work ethic. (The good news is that despite the rules, I also received Truth and love from those at church that kept me on the path of life even through my college years.)

I saw this God of fire as ready to punish me. That was then.

Much remains the same for a vast number of Christians today who have a similar perception of the "God of the Old Testament." Some live by Christian rules to prove their faithfulness and holiness.

During my 20s, millions of people around the world encountered the transforming power of the Holy Spirit in what has been tagged the Charismatic Movement or Charismatic Renewal. It was a spiritual love movement that was in stark contrast to the "free love" culture that burgeoned in America and around the world in the '60s and '70s.

As a Spirit-filled Christian I loved Jesus and welcomed the leading of the Holy Spirit. I sang songs about our God being an awesome God. I know I mentioned His role as Father, but I did not have an understanding of that. Jesus is my personal Savior. That I knew. However, I had no sense of a relationship with Father God. And the Kingdom of God was not talked about. I didn't know this God of fire also has a Kingdom, and that I am part of it.

The Holy Spirit is a great helper, and I avoided sinful things. I loved Jesus and was led by the Spirit and did my best and asked forgiveness when I failed. Then I did my best and asked forgiveness when I failed. Then I did my best and asked forgiveness when....

Then one day everything changed. I had a personal encounter with this holy God, this God of fire.

It happened like this.

After my wife and I had a dramatic encounter with the Holy Spirit in the '70s during grad school in Colorado, our lives became totally focused on listening to the Holy Spirit. We moved to California where I became a high school English teacher. When I wasn't teaching, I was in church. I led the adult Sunday school class, I was an elder, I was the worship leader. I was....well, the pastor called me his Timothy.

Then one day the pastor's wife called me, accusing me of interfering with her son's upcoming marriage. The accusation was false, and as her emotional outburst continued for what seemed forever, my heart was crushed.

She was a mother bear, protecting her cub who had some personal issues. It took many months to get over my deep hurt. Although I understood why she did what she did and forgave her as best I could, the damage was done.

Though I still loved Jesus and was Spirit filled, I felt somehow outside the church even when in church.

Career changes took my wife and me to many different states over the decades. I continued to actively participate in churches wherever we lived, but something was missing. I tried doing certain things such as leading some mentoring and training, but it felt like there was no anointing on it. I didn't understand why.

That brings me to my God encounter.

At the time I was in the middle of another career change in my life. I had resigned my management position in a company to go to grad school again to get an MBA, preparing myself more fully for the next and perhaps final business move before retirement.

My daily routine was to read the Bible and pray in the morning, go to the library in the afternoon to study, and then take the train to downtown Chicago at night to attend classes at DePaul University.

One morning as I sat in the oversized burgundy chair in the front room of our Chicago bungalow, reading the Word and praying, God the Father came up behind me and put His arms around me. He squeezed me. I felt His forearms press into my chest.

It is an understatement to say that when something like that happens, your view of a God of fire shifts dramatically.

Instantly the wound that I had unknowingly carried for 30 years was healed. I had long ago forgiven the person who hurt me, but the wound had remained. For the first time in decades I saw the body of Christ again as real people, precious to the Lord. It's like I re-entered the body of Christ again as a full-fledged member.

For the first time, I knew the Father in a personal, loving way, not just the God of the Old Testament.

At the same moment, I had my identity. I am a son of the Father who loves me.

What a watershed moment.

It is all about love.

It is all about relationship.

It is all about my identity.

My previous understanding of how to be holy because He is holy was shattered.

In Ephesians 1 Paul describes the Divine plan for us to be able to be holy and blameless. He says,

> *Blessed be the God and* **Father** *of our Lord Jesus Christ, who has blessed us with every spiritual blessing in the heavenly places in Christ, just as He (the Father) chose us in Him (Christ) before the foundation of the world,* **that we should be holy and without blame before Him (the Father) in love,** *having predestined us to adoption as sons by Jesus Christ to Himself (the Father), according to the good pleasure of His (our Father's) will, to the praise of the glory of His grace, by which He made us accepted in the Beloved.* (Eph 1:3-6, parenthetical clarifications added)

Our Father had a plan all along for us to be able to be holy as He is holy. He prepared a way for us to be "holy and without blame before Him in love." He had this planned before the world was even created. Imagine, He created earth for us to occupy as His sons and daughters in relationship with Him. He sent His only Beloved Son to die for our sins and restore our relationship to the Father. We are now "accepted in the Beloved."

Wait a minute. The God of fire loves us. He makes it possible to live holy lives as restored children.

My attempts to be holy are no longer necessary. Our own efforts are beside the point. We have a love relationship with our Father. It's relationship, not rules.

One of the biggest results of the Father's hug was that I did not battle as much with temptations. I guess when you live your Christian life trying to do good to please God, you also are more susceptible to the unpleasing works of Satan. When you battle in the flesh to be holy, there seems to be no end to the flesh you have to overcome.

That's not to say I became perfect. We continue to become more like Jesus every day of our lives as we grow in the Father's love. His cleansing fire shines a light on our sins and imperfections AND He provides a way to live a holy life without the condemnation.

In Colossians 1:21-22 Paul explains how Christ makes it possible to stand before our Father as holy:

> *And although you were at one time estranged and alienated and hostile-minded [toward Him], participating in evil things, yet Christ has now reconciled you [to God (the Father)] in His physical body through death, in order to* **present you before the Father holy** *and blameless and beyond reproach.* (Amp, emphasis added)

The holiness the Israelites could not accomplish in their rules and ordinances, we can't accomplish either by trying to follow Christian rules and doing good works. We have already been given holiness because Christ has reconciled us to our Father. He has presented us as holy (set apart) and blameless and beyond reproach (blame and rebuke).

We don't try to be holy. We are holy because He is holy. We don't try to follow rules and ordinances; the Holy Spirit in us leads us in love for our Father as His sons and daughters. We are free to be holy.

When David brings the Ark of the Covenant to Jerusalem with great joy and celebration, he also writes a psalm and gives it to Asaph and the other worship leaders. In this wonderful psalm he proclaims,

> *Give to the Lord the glory due His name; Bring an offering, and come before Him. Oh, worship the Lord in* **the beauty of holiness***!* (1 Chron 16:29)

Imagine that. Holiness is beautiful. As sons and daughters of our Father, we live in an authentic identity, setting us apart from the struggles of religion. That in itself is beautiful. I get to be free to worship and love my Father in a "holy" relationship.

A holy God loves His children who, because of their identity as sons and daughters, can be holy, too.

(Have you noticed the word *identity* repeated? Rick Joyner says the majority of Christians don't know their purpose. I think that is because they don't really understand their identity as the Father's sons and daughters.)

We look more like the Father every day, living in the beauty of holiness. The Holy Spirit continues to transform our lives and actions. We examine ourselves. We want to be a pure and spotless bride at Jesus' return. Our love for Him is so strong we don't want anything to get in the way.

The "fire of God" is coming to people who are able to host His presence, to a holy people. Am I walking in holiness? Do I have any offense against someone? Am I bitter toward someone or about a circumstance? Am I carrying any unforgiveness?

The 50+ prophetic intercession team meets with me weekly. We were talking about how we must first examine ourselves before we judge others. One member said that as she was coming to MorningStar that morning, she was praying, "Lord, show me if I am carrying any bitterness."

Instantly the Holy Spirit brought a person to her mind who had done some hurtful things to her in the past. She thought she had forgiven the person. But she realized that when the Holy Spirit instantly brought the person to her attention, she was still holding some bitterness. She could tell this because she had an emotional reaction to the name. She repented and asked the Lord to forgive her and remove the bitterness.

The Father is cleaning us out, making us holy vessels for His use. Others will see His beauty on us, the beauty of holiness, as we are transformed by His fire.

When the Father hugged me and I recognized my identity as His son, my striving to please Him stopped. My trying to be a perfect Christian ended. It's not about what I do. It's first about who I am. Then the fruit of that identity will come.

I think because there were not others around me who could help me recognize and own sonship with the Father, He came to me to make it clear. It could be, too, I am pretty thick headed and need some remedial attention. Whatever the reason, my life is so much easier to live now. I don't carry religious stress. Do I find myself sometimes trying to do too much Kingdom work and feeling it's not enough? Honestly, there are those times. But when I start my day in prayer and proclaim, "I love you, Father. I love you, Father," I find I get to do Kingdom things; I don't have to do Kingdom things.

Many of those who study the ebb and flow of revivals and great moves of God conclude that when people start to package the move of God in some form, the power leaves. For some reason we think our rational minds know better than God does how to do things. Since the time of Adam and Eve mankind has wanted to be in control, even of God.

We want to define what holiness is and what it looks like. We need to "see" holiness and thus create our own manifestation of its qualities.

It's also because we want to maintain control. We want to get our hands on what God is doing and make sure it keeps going, or we want to make it more palatable to others. Our minds get in the way of our heart.

I read how the Israelites create their own golden calf to worship, even while the fire of God is evident on the mountain where God and Moses are communicating. They quickly adopt the gods of other nations because holiness seems too hard to achieve. It is easier to worship in abominable ways that fulfill their pleasures than to conform to God's directions.

I would never do those things, I say to myself. Yet I have lived through some of the greatest moves of God around the world and have seen the same thing happen in our Christian lives. The Holy Spirit comes in power, and we show off the spiritual gifts and almost turn those who have great spiritual gifts into spiritual rock stars.

If the Old Testament teaches us anything, it teaches us we cannot have any other gods before us. It's like saying to the one who loves you, "I want to marry you, but I just want to keep one girlfriend on the side."

What other gods might we have? What else do we "worship?"

- Is it our own image that we want to present to others, spending hours on our personal appearance and physical look every day?

- Is it our self-righteousness, keeping us feeling spiritually superior because we go to more meetings and listen to more Christian YouTube channels?

- Is it our children, making their love more important than any other love, including that of the Father?

- Is it some false feeling, also known as a wound, which we pamper and dwell on?--People just don't understand me. I pray alone because I can get close to God. People are not important in my life. I don't need to go to church.

- Is it pornography?

- Is it eating habits?

- Is it our critical spirit that makes us feel spiritually superior while putting others down?

Will we ever give up our idols? Will we ever learn? I say, yes.

I know because the Word shows it is possible and I have experienced it. David seems to be the least of the brothers in his family. By everyone's standards he is just a shepherd boy in the background. Yet the Father says David is a man after His own heart. And from David's lineage comes our Lord and Savior.

Our mind, will, and emotions won't keep revivals going. They won't keep us living holy lives. A heart relationship with the Father will, though.

The fire that is coming in a great move of the Father will first cleanse us, His sons and daughters. It is going to remove religious baggage from the past. It will burn away the false notion that we can control our spiritual lives or that we are not worthy to live powerful lives in the future because of past wounds and sins.

It will stamp out our works mentality of having to please Him.

It will prepare us for the Great Harvest.

In the early days of television, "Truth or Consequences" was a very popular program. If the contestant answered falsely by not knowing the answer, he or she suffered the consequences. In general, Americans had a more unified "Christian" understanding of what is right or wrong. They recognized there are consequences for bad behavior. Christian Americans could point to the Old Testament and explain what happens if a people, say, the Israelites, turn from God. Most church-going folks when I grew up could tell you how God wiped out nations who do abominable things. They recognized absolutes and had rules to live by.

Today, those who don't have a relationship with the Father are only left with the rules, and that makes Satan happy. He wants us to believe we can never measure up. He wants to keep us from living in relationship.

God the Father absolutely does have a righteous standard. We know there are consequences, and we'll talk about that some later. However, we are not the Israelites, trying to follow all the laws, failing time and time again. Christ's shed blood on the Cross broke the curse of the law. He restores relationship. His death and resurrection allow us to be reconciled to our Father, not having to prove our love through works.

After the Father hugged me, I no longer felt I had to do things to please Him. I can be holy. I am the offspring of a Holy Father. I am created in His image. I am not an outsider trying to prove my worth.

I am in love with the Father and can approach Him anytime I want because of what His beloved Son Jesus did on the Cross.

Bob Jones, a great modern-day prophet, said, "First it was the time of Jesus. Then it was the time of the Holy Spirit. Now it's going to be the time of the Father."

Those words deeply impacted me because of the Father's hug. The next move is His move!

The Holy Spirit told me the fire of God is coming and **"will cleanse our minds, burning away past sins and failures from remembrance."** As He spoke to me, I envisioned how gold was purified through high temperatures, separating it from the "dross," the waste and imperfections. He is cleaning us up. His fire is going to burn away our failures, our sins from the past that make us feel less than holy. He wants us to be holy just as He is holy.

Later in this book I will talk about specific ways we children of the Father are to prepare for the harvest of souls that is coming. We will explore more how to find and walk in our identity and will talk about areas we will overcome in our lives as a result.

We will be ready because we know who we are as Kingdom sons and daughters, carrying the Father's authority to overcome the evil one and set captives free.

But first I want to introduce you more to the Father who hugged me, allowing me to revel in His love.

Attracted To The Father

The fire of love stops at nothing—it sweeps everything before it. (Sol 8:6 The Message)

How can anyone adequately describe the Father? It's just impossible, it seems. In an earlier manuscript of this book I wrote many chapters trying to help us see and know Him. I gave up. There was too much to say.

When I was in high school in the early '60s, John F. Kennedy was President. He and those around him loved the play, *Camelot*, with King Arthur, Sir Lancelot, and the ideal Knights of the Round Table. At times it seemed the President and his family tried to live a Camelot existence.

He had some of the greatest challenges any president has had to confront. At one point it appeared the United States and the Soviet Union were about to enter World War III because the Soviets were placing ballistic missiles in Cuba. These could easily reach the U.S. only 90 miles away and would be a permanent threat to our safety. The whole world held its collective breath until the Soviet Union backed down and removed the missile threat.

One of the most poignant photos every taken of John F. Kennedy was when his young daughter Carolyn and little son John John were in the Oval Office with him, playing while he dealt with world events. This President, who desired to have an ideal world and had to make life or death decisions for nations, took time from that type of schedule to play with his children.

I somehow see myself in that photo. Father God who holds the world's future in His hands stops for every small Carolyn and every little John John and gives His attention to us, despite all He has to do--because we are His children.

You can know about John F. Kennedy, or, if you are His children, you can live in family relationship with him. It's the same with our Heavenly Father. Anyone can "know" so many things about Him. As His children, however, we see Him differently and personally.

He cares about us in ways we can't comprehend. Though He holds the very world together by the strength of His power, yet He pauses to make certain we are all safe and secure in Him.

The picture of this God of fire seems so incomplete. It's like the proverbial story of the blind men who tried to describe an elephant. One touched its leg and proclaimed the elephant is like a tree. One touched its side and said unequivocally the elephant is like a wall. One grabbed its tail and said the elephant is like a rope.

We all have our partial "touches" of God. I was blinded by my religious past and saw God as a punisher.

Others of us may be blinded because of negative experiences with our own fathers, which we transfer to our impression of our Heavenly Father.

When I was 12, my father died. He was my mother's first love, and their marriage was strong. He seemed like the perfect father to us kids, taking us fishing, going on trips, and so many other things.

Although I received spankings, I only saw his anger once. My father gave my older 13-year-old brother permission to back the station wagon out of the garage. I was excited as I watched him. He backed out, and I opened the driver's door, talking to David. Unfortunately I didn't notice the tree right behind me as he backed up. The tree caught the driver's door and bent the door forward to the front of the car with a screeching sound of bent metal.

Oh, boy. We were in trouble. We had to tell Dad.

We told him, and he came out of the house to see what we were talking about. Then he got mad. "You snots!" he sputtered.

That was it. That was his anger. We didn't even get a spanking.

When my father died, my brother was 15, I was 12, and our baby sister was 4 months old. I remember mom crying every day for the first year after Dad died.

About two years later, another man entered Mom's life. Les was a 40-year-old bachelor who was slow and deliberate. He hadn't been around rambunctious children, and his love for my mom must have blinded him to the consequences of marrying into a family with two teenage boys and a three-year-old girl.

He was so different from my father. My father had been successful in business and was very generous. Although Les was successful, he was also a penny pincher. This didn't sit well with me as a selfish teenager. Besides, who was he to tell us what to do? I treated my stepfather badly.

One of the low points of my teenage life was the day I shamed him into buying me a car to take to college. Fortunately, he knew how to control his temper.

Nine or ten years later, when I was married and had matured, I apologized for the things I had said and done to him. We then became friends, and I saw the gentle and loving side of the man my teenage immaturity had not seen. Les hadn't changed. I had.

I realized he had taken a huge risk marrying my mother. He had given up all his security for love. I started to understand love better.

I think as we look at God the Father, we often see Him through our own distorted prisms. Why did He let this happen to me? Why didn't He answer my prayer? Why doesn't He treat me better? Why? Why? Why?

I counseled a man who had been a Christian for many years. He said he was struggling because he felt he was only about 80% of who he wanted to be. He lived a Spirit-filled life as best he could, but something was missing.

As we talked, he revealed his relationship with his father. "My father was a fiery Irishman," he told me. "He would often get angry and verbally abuse my mother. I rebelled and left home." After his rebellious years, he settled down and grew in the Lord. He is now living a Godly life.

I asked him if his father had ever told him he loved him. The man paused and thought and finally said with emotion, "I never heard him say he loved me." Sadly, this precious Christian had carried a wound since childhood and lived with a distorted impression our Heavenly Father.

We prayed together.

He prayed, forgiving his father. Then he prayed a prayer of repentance for allowing rebellion and judgment to stay in his own life. We then declared the blood of Jesus covers us from all sin and asked the Holy Spirit to replace that personal wound with cleansing. Finally, we bound any imp of Satan that had a legal right to afflict this precious brother because of the judgment he carried against his father, and we told the tormenting spirit where to go. This Spirit-filled man was now smiling. A weight he had carried for decades was now gone. He is now living a greater life of freedom and purpose.

Part of our dilemma in being ready for what's coming is that we may not really know the "God of fire," our Father. He may be different from our past perceptions.

One morning recently I went into our nice food pantry to get my familiar breakfast composed of a protein shake and a banana. I already had ice and water in the blender. The next step was to get a protein shake packet from the third shelf about two-thirds of the way to the back of the pantry.

I reached to pull a protein packet from the box, but the box wasn't there. That seemed odd. I looked on the shelf above and then on the shelf below. Then I started again from the door to closely examine the third shelf. It seemed everything was where it was placed from the day before. I looked at the shelf at the back of the pantry. The box couldn't be there, could it? We keep odds and ends there, a carving knife, some 30-year-old TV trays, used plastic bags from Wal-Mart. The box couldn't be there, but I looked anyway.

Then I became suspicious. My wife Sandy had reorganized the pantry a few weeks earlier. Some pesky moths had made their way into our private castle's food section. She took everything out and put it back in a nicely organized fashion. (After all, I want to know we have a spare bottle of ketchup when the one in the refrigerator runs out.) I thought to myself, "Don't tell me she moved things around again."

I was thinking of asking her, but, like every man, I didn't seek directions. So, I searched the shelves again. The protein box had to be here. I started at the beginning of the shelf again and made my way item by item toward the back, finally getting to the exact spot where I remembered placing the box. There was a box there, but it didn't have the familiar logo of the protein shake company facing me. It had small lettering, probably about the ingredients contained in the box. I thought it was a box of stevia, which we also use to fight the battle of the bulge.

CARRYING THE FATHER'S FIRE

But wait, it was the box containing the protein shakes. It was just turned around. I had simply been looking for a familiar image and couldn't recognize the box in any other way.

I think the same "wrong box" thinking is how we look for many Godly things.

It is one of the reasons the Jews did not recognize Jesus when He came. It's probably why many Christians didn't recognize the move of the Holy Spirit when He swept the world in the '70s and '80s in the Charismatic Movement. They were familiar with a certain way of knowing God. Their minds blinded them to the fact the box has different looks.

This can also be how we think of God the Father. Our ideas of the Old Testament God of creation who was severe in His holiness and punishments blind us to how our Heavenly Father really is. We think we know Him, but we really don't. Christ came to reveal the Father to His own people. They thought they knew what He looked like, but Jesus presented Him in a way their blinded eyes couldn't see.

Our own religious upbringing or current spiritual thoughts or influences from our culture can also blind us to the new way the Father will appear. He can be there right in front of us as the protein box was, but we can't see Him.

The Father is about to make a grand re-appearance in all creation. It may be new and different from what we have known or believed or expected. It will be beyond our familiarity. But we will know it's Him when His refining fire sweeps through our lives to purify us as gold and burn away the dross in our lives. He is coming in "the move of the Father" as Bob Jones and many prophetic voices have indicated. We need eyes that see beyond the familiar in order to identify the new.

So let's look at rediscovering our Father as I did after He hugged me.

After His hug I read the Bible through, substituting the relational term "Father" for "God." It made His autobiography very personal to me and helped me understand my Heavenly Father much, much better.

Step back with me to a time even before the Israelites existed, to the beginning of creation itself to get a better understanding of the Creator.

The history is in His autobiography. His Spirit told men what to write, and through the centuries He organized its compilation and completion.

It starts at the beginning. Can't you just hear Him telling you the story?

"Well, son, in the beginning I created all this, the heaven and the earth. There was really nothing here. You probably never thought about this, but the earth didn't even have a shape. And you wouldn't even know that because you couldn't see it. Darkness was everywhere.

"Of course, because I had a plan that involved you, I took some important creative steps to provide for you even before you were born. I had to separate some things and put them in place and reshape what I saw. I separated the waters so you would have waters under the sky and waters in the sky."

Our Father continues the beginning of His story. He talks about how the land is separated from the waters. He wants us to know about the sun, moon, and stars that capture our attention every day and night we live. He explains where animals and fish come from and all the vegetation on the earth.

Then He gets to His crowning achievement, us, because His autobiography is written for us to read and understand as His offspring. He tells how He formed us, His children, and breathed life into us.

"I made you in my image," He says. "You are in my likeness, both male and female, you all are an earthy manifestation of me. I love you as your Father. I created all these things around you and gave you the authority as my children to care for them because you are so special."

That's just the beginning of Dad's autobiography. There's so, so much more.

Instead of trying to describe this God of fire, our Heavenly Father, let's look at what He writes in His autobiography. The very beginning reveals much of His character as a Father.

At the beginning of creation and of our creation, the Father, our Creator, demonstrates what a Father's heart looks like. We, as all children, are His creation.

A father is responsible for the child's very existence. The Father gives us life itself. Without the Father, we are not alive. Genesis 2:7 says,

And the Lord God (our Father) formed man of the dust of the ground, and breathed into his nostrils the breath of life; and man became a living being.

The Father gives us nourishment and wants us to see beauty all around.

The Lord God (our Father) planted a garden eastward in Eden, and there He put the man whom He had formed. And out of the ground the Lord God (our Father) made every tree grow that is pleasant to the sight and good for food. (Gen 2:8-9)

And the Father gives us choices so our love isn't forced but instead comes from our heart.

The tree of life was also in the midst of the garden, and the tree of the knowledge of good and evil. (Gen 2:9)

The Father also knows we must have purpose, so he gives Adam purpose.

Then the Lord God (our Dad) took the man and put him in the Garden of Eden to tend and keep it. (Gen 2:15)

The Father also wisely instructs His children how to act and warns them about things that will harm them.

And the Lord God (our Papa) commanded the man, saying, "Of every tree of the garden you may freely eat; but of the tree of the knowledge of good and evil you shall not eat, for in the day that you eat of it you shall surely die." (Gen 2:16-17)

Our loving Father also realizes His children must live in relationship to be happy. (Now that is a wise, wise daddy.)

And the Lord God said, "It is not good that man should be alone; I will make him a helper comparable to him." (Gen 2:18)

And Father knew this union was to be special, greater than any other earthly relationship.

Genesis 2:24-25 says,

Therefore a man shall leave his father and mother and be joined to his wife, and they shall become one flesh.

And they were both naked, the man and his wife, and were not ashamed.

With no sin, there is no shame. There is to be no shame in the relationship between a husband and wife.

Some years ago an editorial friend of mine had an open vision. In the vision he was naked, and he tried to cover himself with His hands. The Lord told him to raise his hands and worship Him. My friend protested. The Lord told him again to raise his hands and worship. He finally yielded to the Lord and felt a great release. My friend had been sexually abused by an uncle when he was a child, and the Lord was removing the shame. The Father wants our shame to be gone.

Genesis 3:8-9 continues the story after Adam and Eve sinned:

And they heard the sound of the Lord God (our loving Father) walking in the garden in the cool of the day, and Adam and his wife hid themselves from the presence of the Lord God (their own Dad) among the trees of the garden.

Then the Lord God (Father) called to Adam and said to him, "Where are you?"

The Father meets with His children the first thing each day. That's what good daddies do. But this day would be different.

Genesis 3:10 continues:

So he said, "I heard Your voice in the garden, and I was afraid because I was naked; and I hid myself."

A wise Father knows He has to let His creation make choices. And Adam and Eve make the wrong choice.

They are made in His image. There can be no doubt they are His offspring. Yet they choose something else. The Father knows love can only be real if they choose it for themselves above all the other choices they can make.

The children break the pure father-child relationship. However, the Father does not desert the children who turned against Him.

A popular 18th century religious belief was Deism, the belief that God created the earth and mankind but now sits back and watches it, not getting involved in the day-to-day affairs of man. That's not what our Father's autobiography indicates, however. He was, is, and always will be as close relationally to us as we allow Him to be.

Some people read the Old Testament and conclude, "God is so mean, punishing all those people, even wiping out whole nations?"

I read the Old Testament and conclude, "I can't believe how merciful our Father is. We virtually spit in His face time after time. Yet He plans a way to bring us back together."

He renews His covenant with Israel despite how they rejected Him. Exodus 34:10-11, 24 says,

> *"Behold, I make a covenant. Before all your people I will do marvels such as have not been done in all the earth, nor in any nation; and all the people among whom you are shall see the work of the Lord. For it is an awesome thing that I will do with you. Observe what I command you this day. Behold, I am driving out from before you the Amorite and the Canaanite and the Hittite and the Perizzite and the Hivite and the Jebusite.*
>
> *"I will cast out the nations before you and enlarge your borders."*

To paraphrase the above, the Father says to them, "Just listen to what I tell you, and it will really be good for you."

Our Father will drive the enemy away. He really has gotten a bum wrap. We look at the consequences of man's disobedience and blame the results on God who as Father created us.

He says, "I've never quit loving you and never will. Expect love, love, and more love!" (Jer 31:3, The Message)

This doesn't sound at all like the God who "is a consuming fire," although He is also that. This sounds like a Father who created the heavens and the earth as a place for His offspring, us, to dwell.

For all our Father does for us, we do not have an adequate vocabulary to bless Him back enough, though the psalmist makes a beautiful attempt:

> *Bless the Lord (our Father), O my soul;*
> *And all that is within me, bless His holy name!*

Bless the Lord (our Provider), O my soul,

And forget not all His benefits:

Who forgives all your iniquities,

Who heals all your diseases,

Who redeems your life from destruction,

Who crowns you with lovingkindness and tender mercies,

Who satisfies your mouth with good things,

So that your youth is renewed like the eagle's.

The Lord (our perfect Father) executes righteousness

And justice for all who are oppressed. (Ps 103:1-6)

The Father's children really get special treatment.

Now He is preparing us for what lies ahead. Something dramatic is bursting forth. The move of the Father is upon us. He wants us to be aware of what is now to come. He wants us to be comfortable with His presence. He wants to dwell among us and with us. Simply put, He wants to love us like a father. He is going to take us places the Church has not gone before. I am writing this book to help us get ready.

Just as He speaks to Adam and Eve in the garden, He speaks directly to many others.

He speaks to Moses when the bush is on fire but doesn't burn up. He continues to audibly direct his steps as he takes the Israelites through the wilderness.

Before the Israelites enter the Promised Land, Moses reviews how they themselves had heard from God. Moses reminds them,

The Lord said to me, 'Gather the people to Me, and I will let them hear My words, that they may learn to fear Me all the days they live on the earth, and that they may teach their children.'

Then you came near and stood at the foot of the mountain, and the mountain burned with fire to the midst of heaven, with darkness, cloud, and thick darkness. And the Lord spoke to you out of the midst of the fire. You heard the sound of the words, but saw no form; you only heard a voice. So He declared to you His covenant, which He commanded you to perform, the Ten Commandments; and He wrote them on two tablets of stone. (Deut 4:10-13)

Later, the Father speaks to David, who enquires of Him before going to battle.

He speaks to the prophets, giving the words to say to kings and people alike.

His autobiography continues to unfold as we turn to the New Covenant. What this Holy God, this God of fire, does next is amazing.

The Son Reveals The Father

"Most assuredly, I say to you, the Son can do nothing of Himself, but what He sees the Father do; for whatever He does, the Son also does in like manner. For the Father loves the Son, and shows Him all things that He Himself does."
(Jn 5:19-20)

Wait a minute. I thought Jesus was everything. He can do anything. I grew up singing "Jesus loves me, this I know." I even sang it to Santa Claus when as a three-year-old I sat on his lap in the Woolworth department store in Wausau, Wisconsin. He asked if I could sing a song, and I delivered.

I heard about Jesus a lot growing up in our church. Of course the Holy Spirit was mentioned, too. We were told Jesus is our example. We are to follow Jesus. We are to live the way He lived. I tried!

I never heard John 5:19-20 until I was many decades older. Jesus looks to the Father. What is He doing? Jesus will do the same thing.

Well if it's good enough for Jesus, it must be good enough for us.

The following verses unveil the beautiful love connection they have for each other:

The Father loves the Son, and shows Him all things that He Himself does. (Jn 5:20)

(The Father) committed all judgment to the Son, that all should honor the Son just as they honor the Father. He who does not honor the Son does not honor the Father who sent Him. (Jn 5:22-23)

So, as I was growing up, I didn't totally miss it. We did honor the Son. We just didn't understand the God of love the way Jesus did.

The Father speaks His language of love over His Son several times in the New Testament portion of His autobiography. As Jesus is baptized, the Father's voice fills the atmosphere, "You are My beloved Son; in You I am well pleased." (Luke 3:22) He breaks the Old Covenant beliefs of works and duties and traditions. He talks about love.

This Father's heart is so incredibly big. From the very beginning He has a plan to bring us back into His household. His love for us is so immense that He sends His Son on the greatest rescue mission of all time, even though it costs His loved beloved Son His life.

There's something about this Father-Son relationship that can't be fully understood by sinful man. How could a Father allow His Son to endure such pain and suffering? How could a Son be so in love and union with His Father that He will gladly sacrifice His own life for the good of the mission? Yes, the New Testament contains a riveting love story. And we are in the middle of it.

When reading the New Testament after the Father hugged me, I changed the word *God* to *Father*, just as I had done in the Old Testament. (I know this does not always make theological sense, but it broke my narrow understanding of God.) The New Testament reveals much, much more about my Heavenly Father in a personal and powerful and relational way.

In many of the verses of Scripture that follow in this book, I will continue to substitute the word *Father* for *God,* putting parentheses around the substitution, or I will place relational words such as *Father* or *Dad* in parentheses after the word *God.*

The Gospels are especially revelatory about our Father because one of Jesus' goals for coming to earth in the first place is to reveal the Father.

Right after the Father speaks over His Son at His baptism, Jesus fasts and prays in the wilderness for 40 days and is tempted by Satan himself. He tempts Jesus by referring to His identity as the Father's Son. Satan recognizes the relationship of Father and Son. Jesus' defense in all these temptations is to recognize the authority, prominence, and power of His Father but not to act as God. Rather He resists fully as man, showing that a man who is full of the Father's love can withstand any temptation. We can do the same. The more of the Father's love we possess, the more power we have to overcome Satan.

The Israelites' perception of a fearful God is being shattered. When He speaks to them on Mount Sinai, they tremble, crying out to Moses, "You speak with us, and we will hear; but let not God speak with us, lest we die." (Ex 20:19)

Our God of the New Testament tenderly speaks as a Father over Jesus. "This is my Son." And the crowd hears a Father's heart.

Early in His ministry Jesus explains the Father's love to Nicodemus (and to us).

This is how much (our Father) loved the world: He gave his Son, his one and only Son. And this is why: so that no one need be destroyed; by believing in him, anyone can have a whole and lasting life. (Jn 3:16, The Message)

This is not a God who uses His power to make us live by laws and rules or to scare people out of hell. He wants to love us into the Kingdom.

That is Jesus' message, too. Jesus doesn't come just to save sinners. He comes to reunite us to our Father and His Kingdom. Our self-centered western view of Christ's purpose puts us at the center of Jesus' affection. We say, "If I were the only one, Jesus would have died for me." Well, maybe. But it's not about us and the benefits we receive by being saved. It's much, much more. Love reaches out. It's about eternal love and our reconnection to our Father and to His Kingdom purposes.

Jesus speaks and heals, revealing the Kingdom. The people in Galilee hear His gracious words and see the miracles, and some want Him to stay right there to keep the revival going. But Jesus says, "I must preach the kingdom of (the Father) to the other cities also, because for this purpose I have been sent." (Luke 4:43)

He is changing their vision and how they see things around them, just as He wants us to see differently. It's a new way of life. He tells them the pure in heart will see the Father and peacemakers will be called "sons of (the Father)." He says those who are persecuted for righteousness' sake will inherit the "kingdom of heaven."

His comments are radically different from what the Jews are used to hearing. Jesus is introducing something beyond the Law and the way people perceive God. Jesus tells the crowds to do charitable deeds in secret, "and your Father who sees in secret will Himself reward you openly." (Matt 6:4) What? God is so interested in us that He sees even the little things? He is as close to us as an ideal earthly father could be? He wants to bless us as any loving father does? Yes. Yes. Yes.

Now that's different. And the Father's autobiography gets more exciting and personal.

Early in His ministry Jesus takes a defining action that clearly reveals His relationship to the Father and how the Father's Son will act. It is also a prophetic picture of how we are to be.

Matthew 21:12-14 describes the incident this way:

Then Jesus went into the temple of God and drove out all those who bought and sold in the temple, and overturned the tables of the money changers and the seats of those who sold doves. And He said to them, "It is written, 'My house shall be called a house of prayer,' but you have made it a 'den of thieves.'"

Then the blind and the lame came to Him in the temple, and He healed them.

Jesus wants a dwelling place for the Father. He wants the temple cleansed and turned back to a house of prayer, a place of communion and communication with the Father. Why? Because He wants the same for us. He isn't just having a cleaned out building. He is giving a prophetic symbol for what we are to look like. The fire of God is coming to our own personal temples to clean out the moneychangers and any other counterfeit Christianity we possess. Then we will be able to heal others.

The perfect Son is revealing a perfect Father who wants to bring us back into relationship.

Would you like to know the Father better? Here's what you do. Read the Gospels through, looking for the Father. Before you read, ask Him to reveal Himself in the Scriptures. You will see Him behind all of Jesus' actions. You will understand He calls you to the same love relationship He has with His Son.

You will see He is not the feared God I thought of when I sang "Holy, Holy, Holy" in church years ago. This isn't a God who is looking to punish anyone who slips up. He is our personal and active Father, a Heavenly Father who cares for us, watches us, and blesses us. And, yes, He is holy, too.

Jesus tells His followers, "Your Father knows the things you have need of before you ask Him." (Matt 6:8)

Then Jesus leads them in prayer, starting with, "Our Father." (Matt 6:9)

Jesus connects them (and us) relationally to a Father, shattering the incomplete image of God as they understood Him. Matthew 6:8-13 records Jesus' conversation:

Your Father knows the things you have need of before you ask Him. In this manner, therefore, pray:
> *Our Father in heaven,*
> *Hallowed be Your name.*
> *Your kingdom come.*
> *Your will be done*
> *On earth as it is in heaven.*
> *Give us this day our daily bread.*
> *And forgive us our debts,*
> *As we forgive our debtors.*
> *And do not lead us into temptation,*
> *But deliver us from the evil one.*

For Yours is the kingdom and the power and the glory forever. Amen.

Jesus' prayer reveals many of the Father's attributes—

- He is our Father.
- He has a Kingdom.
- He has a plan to be completed here on earth just as He does in heaven.
- The Father will guide us so we don't yield to the wrong things.
- And He has the power to keep us out of harm's way, which the devil would like to bring upon us.
- Then Jesus praises this marvelous Father--our Father

has a Kingdom, He has power, and the ultimate glory is His, not just now but forever.

This is Jesus' Father and our Father also.

Jesus sends His disciples out under the Father's authority to demonstrate kingdom life. He tells them, "As you go, preach, saying, 'The kingdom of heaven is at hand.' Heal the sick, cleanse the lepers, raise the dead, cast out demons. Freely you have received, freely give." (Matt 10:7-8) He has authorized us to do the same. Some of us just didn't realize we live in sonship with the Father.

The fourth chapter of the Gospel of John records Jesus talking to the woman at the well while the disciples are away buying something to eat. When they return, they urge Jesus to eat. But Jesus says, "I have food to eat of which you do not know."

The perplexed disciples ask among themselves, "Has anyone brought Him anything to eat?"

Jesus says to them,

My food is to do the will of Him who sent Me, and to finish His work. Do you not say, "There are still four months and then comes the harvest"? Behold, I say to you, lift up your eyes and look at the fields, for they are already white for harvest! And he who reaps receives wages, and gathers fruit for eternal life, that both he who sows and he who reaps may rejoice together. (John 4:34-36)

Jesus' utmost fulfillment is in carrying out the Father's plan. He is given the authority to finish the work, which in this case is to be the sacrifice that allows us all to become sons and daughters of God the Father. Jesus tells His disciples they too are to carry out the Father's will by bringing many more children into the Father's household as our Father desires.

Now, at the end of the age, the harvest is upon us. The fields are, indeed, ripe. Our Father is bringing His fire to set us ablaze to be able to handle the harvest that is here.

Bringing in the harvest sometimes cost the disciples everything. It sometimes costs us a lot, too. The harvest can even be in our own homes. The deepest desire in any of us parents is to see our children surrendered to the Lord. Right now that may not be the reality. But even in that the Father shares hope because He has had the same issue.

Here's how He handled it.

We all know the story of the prodigal well. It is told in the fifteenth chapter of the Gospel of Luke. A father has two children who have everything a child could want. The Father is very wealthy and gladly shares all he has with his children. But that isn't enough for the sons.

The youngest wants to selfishly consume the father's blessings and says to his dad, "Father, give me the portion of goods that falls to me." The father divides his own livelihood and gives it to each of the sons. (Luke 15:12)

The younger son takes off and wastes it all, living a selfish, sinful life. Finally, when he has lost everything and is in desperate straits, he "came to himself" Luke 15:17 says. He then thinks of his father and his generosity, even to the servants. It seems his father's example and demonstrated love have made a permanent impression on the young man.

He heads home with his memorized repentance speech running through his mind. As he reaches the property, the father, who has been watching for his son's return all this time, runs out to his son and hugs and kisses him. Before the son can even speak, this mature father speaks love for his son through his actions.

Then the son speaks his practiced remarks into his father's ears. "Father, I have sinned against heaven and in your sight, and am no longer worthy to be called your son." (Luke 15:21)

This wise father does not remind the son how bad he has been, the foolish choices he has made, the unacceptable lifestyle he has lived. Instead he celebrates the return and throws a party because his loved son was brought back to life and identity.

The story continues. The other son has also been given his inheritance at the same time the younger son received his. But there is something wrong with his heart and motives also. He becomes jealous because the prodigal's return is celebrated.

I'm sure the wise father knows this older son's heart, even before he complains. It seems he wants more also. He wants to be celebrated as being the faithful son. He selfishly wants the father to spoil him by throwing parties for him because he has stayed home. The wise father did not do this.

Instead he leads by example, showing the older son who always had everything that goods don't matter, parties don't matter. What matters is a demonstration of real love and acceptance.

In the end, this father reaches both sons in their very different ways of life and mindsets. The story, after all, is about our Father and His powerful, never changing, and righteous love for His children.

The story is another example to us 50+ers that as we stand steadfast and model a loving lifestyle, our children will see it and live lives that take them into a greater identity.

We 50+ers will emulate how the Father sees and lovingly waits for any prodigal's return, knowing it will happen. We will call our children and the next generation into their purpose and calling. That is what we get to do as fathers and mothers in the Lord.

When Jesus tells the story, He is revealing His own Father's heart for His own prodigal gentiles to return home so He can shower them with love. Jesus is also saying the Jews, who have everything but are not appreciative, will one day come to their senses when the prodigals return and they all live under the Father's broad and fertile, prosperous, and loving roof.

I think He is revealing His heart for me also. I, like the prodigal, have not always recognized the precious nature of the Father's spiritual gifts and squandered them in my own loose charismatic lifestyle. I am also like the other son who stays home. How many times have thought I knew more and was special and then judged others? Oh, Lord, we have a lot to learn.

I know, however, the Father has called us for just such a time as this to make a difference, to be the Joshuas and Calebs, walking in wisdom, health, and maturity in identity as sons and daughters of the Father--leading the next generation into their promised land.

We can live in a love relationship with the Father just as Jesus did. The Son lives in the Father's love and will do anything for the Father because that love is so strong. Jesus describes that love to His disciples in John 14:27-31, saying,

> *Peace I leave with you; my peace I give you. I do not give to you as the world gives. Do not let your hearts be troubled and do not be afraid.*
>
> *You heard me say, "I am going away and I am coming back to you." If you loved me, you would be glad that I am going to the Father, for the Father is greater than I. I have told you now before it happens, so that when it does happen you will believe. I will not say much more to you, for the prince of this world is coming.* **He has no hold over me***, but he comes so that the world may learn that I love the Father and do exactly what my Father has commanded me.* (NIV, emphasis added)

Jesus is clean in spirit, soul, and body. Satan cannot hold Him from His purpose. He has "no hold over" Him. And Satan has no hold over us either. We are sons and daughters of the Father. We obey out of love. We are on fire with God.

So, what is our purpose?

- Is it to save a million people,
- is it to write the world's greatest Christian book,
- is it to be wildly and accurately prophetic,
- is it to heal people?

I think it is the same as Jesus' purpose, to glorify the Father's name. In a deep relationship with our Father, He will be glorified as we do what He directs us to do.

Just before Jesus is betrayed, He speaks to His Father, saying,

I have glorified You on the earth. I have finished the work which You have given Me to do. (Jn 17:4)

Isn't that what we want to do, too?

The evening He was betrayed, Jesus tells the disciples more about their Father:

The Father Himself loves you, because you have loved Me, and have believed that I came forth from God. I came forth from the Father and have come into the world. Again, I leave the world and go to the Father. (Jn 16:27-28)

After His resurrection, Jesus sees Mary by His tomb. She, supposing Him to be the gardener, says to Him,

"Sir, if You have carried Him away, tell me where You have laid Him, and I will take Him away."

Jesus said to her, "Mary!"

She turned and said to Him, "Rabboni!" (which is to say, Teacher).

Jesus said to her, "Do not cling to Me, for I have not yet ascended to My Father; but go to My brethren and say to them, 'I am ascending to My Father and your Father, and to My God and your God.' "

Mary Magdalene came and told the disciples that she had seen the Lord, and that He had spoken these things to her. (Jn 20:15-18)

After Jesus' resurrection, His disciples begin understanding the message. The Father, the Creator of heaven and earth, the God of the now "New Testament," is our Father and loves us.

Before Jesus ascends to heaven, He tells His followers one final thing about His Father, saying,

Behold, I send the Promise of My Father upon you; but tarry in the city of Jerusalem until you are endued with power from on high. (Luke 24:49)

Our Father gives us yet another gift, as though giving His Son for our restoration weren't enough. Our Dad sends the Holy Spirit to equip His new sons and daughters and us, giving us power to walk in Kingdom life and live daily in His love and purpose as His sons and daughters.

The new church gets to be an ambassador of the Kingdom as sons and daughters of the Father, filled with the Holy Spirit.

The New Church And
The God Of Love

For now we see in a mirror, dimly, but then face to face.
Now I know in part, but then I shall know just as I also
am known.

And now abide faith, hope, love, these three; but the greatest
of these is love. (1 Cor 13:12-13)

I t's obvious the early church gets the message of love. They go about healing people just as Jesus did--what He saw the Father doing. "I am the Lord who heals you," the Father declared to the Israelites centuries earlier.

Paul and the other apostles understand their relationship with the Father as well as with Jesus. Most of the New Testament epistles begin with that recognition. Notice the references to the Father in the salutation of some of Paul's letters.

Grace to you and peace from **God our Father** *and the Lord Jesus Christ. (Rom 1:7)*

Grace to you and peace from **God our Father** *and the Lord Jesus Christ.* (1 Cor 1:3)

Paul, an apostle of Jesus Christ by the will of God, and Timothy our brother, To the church of God which is at Corinth, with all the saints who are in all Achaia: Grace to you and peace from **God our Father** *and the Lord Jesus Christ.* (2 Cor 1:1-2)

Paul, an apostle (not from men nor through man, but through Jesus Christ and **God the Father** *who raised Him from the dead), and all the brethren who are with me, To the churches of Galatia: Grace to you and peace from* **God the Father** *and our Lord Jesus Christ.* (Gal 1:1-3)

Paul, an apostle of Jesus Christ by the will of God, To the saints who are in Ephesus, and faithful in Christ Jesus: Grace to you and peace from **God our Father** *and the Lord Jesus Christ.* (Eph 1:1-2)

"God," as the Jewish nation knew Him and as gentiles were learning, is now defined as "Father."

Paul is comfortable in His relationship with the Father in all his epistles. Throughout his epistles, Paul loves talking about the Father and His love and relationship with us.

As an example, in Colossians Paul prays they might be filled with the knowledge of the Father's will "in all wisdom and spiritual understanding." He also wants them to be fruitful and to increase "in the knowledge of (the Father)." (Col 1:9-10)

He continues to pray they would be "strengthened with all might, according to His (the Father's) glorious power, for all patience and long suffering with joy."

Then Paul thanks the Father:

Giving thanks to the Father who has qualified us to be partakers of the inheritance of the saints in the light. He (the Father) has delivered us from the power of darkness and conveyed us into the kingdom of the Son of His love, in whom we have redemption through His blood, the forgiveness of sins. (Col 1:12-14)

Yes, the Father's plan, which was carried out in Christ's sacrifice, qualifies us to come back into the family. We have gone from darkness to light. And we get to live in the Kingdom of His Son.

The Father's autobiography reveals more about Him and His love for us the more we read it.

Other New Testament writers agree with what Paul says, and they amplify thoughts about our love relationship with the Father.

John, the disciple who rested on Jesus' breast, understands love. He becomes an authority on love, as his epistles demonstrate. He knows the Father well.

He starts 1 John, showing the connection between Jesus and the Father.

That which was from the beginning, which we have heard, which we have seen with our eyes, which we have looked upon, and our hands have handled, concerning the Word of life—the life was manifested, and we have seen, and bear witness, and declare to you that eternal life which was with the Father and was manifested to us—that which we have seen and heard we declare to you, that you also may have fellowship with us; and truly **our fellowship is with the Father and with His Son Jesus Christ**. *And these things we write to you that your joy may be full.*

This is the message which we have heard from Him and declare to you, that **God (the Father) is light** *and in Him is no darkness at all.* (1 Jn 1:1-5)

And if we do something wrong, Jesus helps us restore our relationship with our Father. Sometimes you need an older brother to help you out, as 1 John 2:1 says,

My little children, these things I write to you, so that you may not sin. And if anyone sins, we have an Advocate with the Father, Jesus Christ the righteous.

Our love for the Father and Son should separate us from the love of the world. First John 2:15-17 puts it this way.

Do not love the world or the things in the world. If anyone loves the world, the love of the Father is not in him. For all that is in the world—the lust of the flesh, the lust of the eyes, and the pride of life—is not of the Father but is of the world. And the world is passing away, and the lust of it; but he who does the will of God (our Father) abides forever.

Choosing the love from the Father gives us eternal life.

John also restates in his own words what Jesus said—he who has seen Me has seen the Father. John says it this way,

Therefore let that abide in you which you heard from the beginning. If what you heard from the beginning abides in you, you also will **abide in the Son and in the Father.** *And this is the promise that He has promised us—eternal life.* (Jn 2:24-25)

John can't overstate the Father's love, proclaiming,

Behold what manner of love the Father has bestowed on us, that we should be called children of God (the Father)! Therefore the world does not know us, because it did not know Him. Beloved, now we are children of God (our Father). (1 Jn 3:1-2)

If we receive the Father's love, we are empowered to walk in that love. After all, we are sons and daughters of our loving Father. People will know us by our love, as John says,

> In this the children of (the Father) and the children of the devil are manifest: Whoever does not practice righteousness is not of (our Father), nor is he who does not love his brother. For this is the message that you heard from the beginning, that we should love one another. (1 Jn 3:10-11)

And he repeats the message, which is central to who we are and how we should live.

> Beloved, let us love one another, for love is of God (our Father); and everyone who loves is born of (the Father) and knows (the Father). He who does not love does not know (our Dad), for (our Dad) is love. In this the love of (our Father) was manifested toward us, that God (the Father) has sent His only begotten Son into the world, that we might live through Him. In this is love, not that we loved (the Father), but that He loved us and sent His Son to be the propitiation for our sins. Beloved, if (our Father) so loved us, we also ought to love one another. (1 Jn 4:7-11)

And he continues,

> No one has seen (the Father) at any time. If we love one another, (the Father) abides in us, and His love has been perfected in us. By this we know that we abide in Him, and He in us, because He has given us of His Spirit. And we have seen and testify that the Father has sent the Son as Savior of the world. Whoever confesses that Jesus is the Son of (the Father), (the Father) abides in him, and he in (the Father). And we have known and believed the love that (our loving Father) has for us. (Our Father) is love, and he who abides

in love abides in (the Father), and (the Father) in him. (1 Jn 4:12-16)

Imagine, the Father's DNA is our DNA. We all look like the same family.

He doesn't just take us in off the streets and clean us up and feed us and give us a nice bedroom. He doesn't then adopt us and help us live in His house with His family name. Oh, no. That's not it. It's much more. We are born again. We are a new creation whose spirit is joined with His Spirit. It's an utter transformation, not just a clean-up act.

We now have access to all He provides because we are eternal sons and daughters, the carriers of His presence and nature. Old thing have passed away; they are dead. We have become a new creation with eternal Godly characteristics and DNA!!

The Father's fiery love then continues to cleanse and purify us, shaping and equipping us. The spiritual reality of the Father's love gives us understanding of all spiritual things, including the plots and ploys of Satan our enemy.

Love wins. No matter what we face or endure, we win when we are in the Father's love. That love also separates us from the world and puts us in opposition to the enemy of our souls. Before the Father's love was poured into our hearts, we were captives to Satan and the fallen world. Now we live eternally in union with our Father and our wonderful Savior Jesus in all circumstances.

On the evening of His arrest, Jesus warns His disciples about what is coming to all of them, telling them, "In the world you will have tribulation; but be of good cheer, I have overcome the world." (Jn 16:33)

Peter hears it. Later, as one of the chief apostles who develops an intimate love of the Father, he warns the Church of what is happening in the world:

Beloved, do not think it strange concerning the fiery trial which is to try you, as though some strange thing happened to you; but rejoice to the extent you partake of Christ's sufferings, that when His glory is revealed, you may also be glad with exceeding joy. If you are reproached for the name of Christ, blessed are you, for the Spirit of glory and of (the Father) rests upon you. (1 Pet 4:12-14)

The Father's love doesn't free us from life's issues; it gives us strength to endure and overcome whatever comes our way. In Paul's great love chapter, 1 Corinthians 13, he spiritually defines love, including,

Love suffers long and is kind; love does not envy; love does not parade itself, is not puffed up; does not behave rudely, does not seek its own, is not provoked, thinks no evil; does not rejoice in iniquity, but rejoices in the truth; **bears all things**, *believes all things, hopes all things,* **endures all things.**

Love never fails. (I Cor 13:4-8)

Our love relationship as sons and daughters of the Father gives us the courage and strength to "bear" and "endure all things."

This eternal love relationship with the Father also gives us the power to recognize the devil, resist him, and overcome him. Peter elaborates on the spiritual battle resulting from our Godly love. He tells fellow Christians,

Be sober, be vigilant; because your adversary the devil walks about like a roaring lion, seeking whom he may devour. Resist him, steadfast in the faith, knowing that the same sufferings are experienced by your brotherhood in the world. But may the God of all grace (that is, our Heavenly Father), who called us to His eternal glory by Christ Jesus, after you have suffered a while, perfect, establish, strengthen, and settle you. (1 Pet 5:8-10)

In the reality of our spiritual fight the Father will perfect us and establish us and give us more strength for the tasks and situations and even calm and settle us.

The more we get to know the Father and grow in our love relationship, the more confident we become that we are maturing, ready to take on what comes our way. We love the Father and realize He is glorious and has everything under control and always will.

"God is love," John proclaims in 1 John 4:8. The Father is love. He doesn't just have love for us. He IS love. He wants to consume us in His love.

In Paul's letter to the Galatians, he encourages them not to look at rules and traditions or to judge each other by their cultural or religious backgrounds. He calls them to unity in love. And he has a remarkable clause explaining how to bring this about, how to be overcomers, how to have the faith to change lives and set the captives free, to bring healing and deliverance.

Paul says in Galatians 5:6 that **faith works through love**. When we are consumed by the Father's love, we have the faith to move mountains.

This fiery God is pouring on us the fire of love that purifies and perfects us. We are being transformed into Love Himself. That transformation gives us the faith to believe all things are possible.

Bonus material: Drilling down for more

I hope you are sensing and embracing the important relationship we have with the Father. If you want to go a little deeper, continue reading here. Or, go to the next chapter. I am about to quote many verses of Scripture, and it may slow your reading pleasure, but they will more clearly illustrate the Father.

Let's look at the Apostle Paul's revelation of the Father in Ephesians.

Paul's time in Ephesus is very important. Acts 19:9-10 records that Paul reasoned "daily in the school of Tyrannus. And this continued for two years, so all who dwelt in Asia heard the word of the Lord Jesus, both Jews and Greeks." Paul's important teaching in this powerful pagan city, which worships the goddess Diana, influences all of Asia.

In his letter to the Ephesians Paul explains the Father's eternal plan in detail. I remember reading Ephesians right after I was filled with the Spirit in 1972, during the great move of the Holy Spirit in what we began calling the Charismatic Movement. This letter, which I had read earlier in my Christian life, now came alive. The words seemed to jump off the page as I read them. It talks about who Jesus really is. It explains our connections to God, to the Holy Spirit, and to each other. It helps us see the body of Christ and how to be united in love. What exciting reading.

But I missed something critical. I didn't perceive the Father's central role in all that was said in this wonderful epistle. Now I see more clearly.

The first chapter begins by identifying the Father.

Grace to you and peace from God our Father and the Lord Jesus Christ. (Eph 1:2)

Paul has a personal identity and relationship with God, saying He is **our** Father.

Paul is in awe of God, our Father. In verse 3 he proclaims to the Ephesians,

Blessed and worthy of praise be the God and Father *of our Lord Jesus Christ, who has blessed us with every spiritual blessing in the heavenly realms in Christ.* (Amp)

Then he continues to talk about our Father, how He has planned our welfare and how the sacrifice of His Son takes us to heavenly places as sons and daughters of the Father.

Let's look at some of Paul's revelation of the Father in verses 4 through 14 of the first chapter of Ephesians.

[in His love] He (the Father) chose us in Christ [actually selected us for Himself as His own] before the foundation of the world, so that we would be holy [that is, consecrated, set apart for Him, purpose-driven] and blameless in His sight. (Amp.)

Imagine that, our Father had us in mind before the world even existed. And He planned for us to be united with Him in a holy and blameless relationship. Now that's an extraordinary Father.

In love He (our Father) predestined and lovingly planned for us to be adopted to Himself as [His own] children through Jesus Christ, in accordance with the kind intention and good pleasure of His will—to the praise of His glorious grace and favor, which He so freely bestowed on us in the Beloved [His Son, Jesus Christ]. (Amp.)

From His heart of love our loving Father planned for our adoption by sending His own beloved Son to be a sacrifice for our sins.

In Him we have redemption [that is, our deliverance and salvation] through His blood, [which paid the penalty for our sin and resulted in] the forgiveness and complete pardon of our sin, in accordance with the riches of His grace which He lavished on us. (Amp.)

Jesus' personal sacrifice and shed blood made it possible for us to be forgiven and connected once again to the Father.

In all wisdom and understanding [with practical insight] He made known to us the mystery of His (the Father's) will according to His good pleasure, which He purposed in Christ, with regard to the fulfillment of the times [that is, the end of history, the climax of the ages]—to bring all things together in Christ, [both] things in the heavens and things on the earth. (Amp.)

The Father then revealed to us the mystery of His own will. We, as sons and daughters of the Father, are joined in Christ for eternal purposes. We are people of purpose!

In Him also we have received an inheritance [a destiny—we were claimed by God (our Father) as His own], having been predestined (chosen, appointed beforehand) according to the purpose of Him who works everything in agreement with the counsel and design of His will, so that we who were the first to hope in Christ [who first put our confidence in Him as our Lord and Savior] would exist to the praise of His glory. (Amp.)

Now we have an inheritance because we are sons and daughters of the Father. Now we are living manifestations of the Father's plan. Everyone should praise the Father for His plan.

In Him, you also, when you heard the word of truth, the good news of your salvation, and [as a result] believed in Him, were stamped with the seal of the promised Holy Spirit [the One promised by Christ] as owned and protected [by God]. The Spirit is the guarantee [the first installment, the pledge, a foretaste] of our inheritance until the redemption of God's own [purchased] possession [His believers], to the praise of His glory. (Amp.)

And another thing. When we accept Jesus' sacrifice for our sins, we are given the Holy Spirit to help us realize who we are. Our inheritance comes right from the Father. We are owned and protected by our Father!

Paul is so thankful for the Ephesian Christians. He says,

I also, after I heard of your faith in the Lord Jesus and your love for all the saints, do not cease to give thanks for you, making mention of you in my prayers: that **the God of our Lord Jesus Christ, the Father of glory,** *may give to you the spirit of wisdom and revelation in the knowledge of Him, the eyes of your understanding being enlightened; that you may know what is the hope of His calling, what are the riches of the glory of His inheritance in the saints, and what is the exceeding greatness of His power toward us who believe, according to the working of His mighty power which He worked in Christ when He raised Him from the dead.* (Eph 1:15-20)

We will receive wisdom and revelation in the knowledge of our Father. As we grow up in Christ, we will see how rich we are as sons and daughters. This is our Father who raised His Son from the dead.

I need to add a parenthesis here. Although I want us to have a revelation of the Father, I do not want to diminish our revelation of our Lord and Savior Jesus. He is over all things in the Church, His body. He is the head. We get our direction from Him. Jesus made us alive again by His sacrifice. He sits at the right hand of the Father.

Paul's goal in all he does ties directly to his Lord and Savior. Philippians 3:7-11 expresses it powerfully.

What things were gain to me, these I have counted loss for Christ. Yet indeed I also count all things loss for the excellence of the knowledge of Christ Jesus my Lord, for whom I have suffered the loss of all things, and count them as rubbish, that I may gain Christ and be found in Him, not having my own righteousness, which is from the law, but that which is through faith in Christ, the righteousness which is from (the Father) by faith; that I may know Him and the power of His resurrection, and the fellowship of His sufferings, being conformed to His death, if, by any means, I may attain to the resurrection from the dead.

He continues. *The Message* translation of Philippians 3:12-16 states Paul's words in our vernacular:

I'm not saying that I have this all together, that I have it made. But I am well on my way, reaching out for Christ, who has so wondrously reached out for me. Friends, don't get me wrong: By no means do I count myself an expert in all of this, but I've got my eye on the goal, where (the Father) is beckoning us onward—to Jesus. I'm off and running, and I'm not turning back.

So let's keep focused on that goal, those of us who want everything (the Father) has for us. If any of you have something else in mind, something less than total commitment, (the Father) will clear your blurred vision—you'll see it yet! Now that we're on the right track, let's stay on it.

Paul realizes the Father's plan is for us to look like Jesus.

So, let's now get back to Ephesians and some more remarkable characteristics of our loving Father from Ephesian 2:4-9:

But (our Father), who is rich in mercy, because of His great love with which He loved us, even when we were dead in trespasses, made us alive together with Christ (by grace you have been saved), and raised us up together, and made us sit together in the heavenly places in Christ Jesus, that in the ages to come He might show the exceeding riches of His grace in His kindness toward us in Christ Jesus. For by grace you have been saved through faith, and that not of yourselves; it is the (the Father's gift), not of works, lest anyone should boast.

The Father's great love brings us back to Himself through His Son. It is His gift to us. Nothing we can do on our own will accomplish that.

We are His workmanship, as Ephesians 2:10 says:

For we are His (the Father's) workmanship, created in Christ Jesus for good works, which God (our Father) prepared beforehand that we should walk in them.

We together as the body are a temple in which the Father dwells, Ephesians 2:21-22 proclaims:

The whole building, being fitted together, grows into a holy temple in the Lord, in whom you also are being built together for a dwelling place of God (the Father) in the Spirit.

If I keep writing about Paul's revelation of the Father's role and plan for us he shows just in Ephesians, I will have to quote almost the entire letter. So, I have to let you do that yourself.

Remember how in John 12:28 Jesus prays that the Father will be glorified? Paul prays the same thing--"to Him (our Father) be the glory in the church and in Christ Jesus." (Eph 3:21)

Finally, Paul admonishes the Ephesian church in Ephesian 5:1-2:

Therefore become imitators of God (our Father) [copy Him and follow His example], as well-beloved children [imitate their father]; and walk continually in love [that is, value one another—practice empathy and compassion, unselfishly seeking the best for others], just as Christ also loved you and gave Himself up for us, an offering and sacrifice to God [slain for you, so that it became] a sweet fragrance. (Amp.)

Jesus said He only does what He sees the Father doing (Jn 5:19). The same is true for us, the children of the same loving, powerful, fiery, compassionate Father.

A Spoonful Of Sugar

Do not withhold correction from a child,
For if you beat him with a rod, he will not die.
You shall beat him with a rod,
And deliver his soul from hell. (Prov 23:13-14)

Infants learn quickly how to get what they want. Early cries get quick responses from loving parents who want their little bundle to be comfortable. I don't know exactly how long it takes for these little cherubs to reverse the stimulus-response principle. But I do know they all develop ways to get their desires met, training their parents to respond to their selfish needs.

Little boys, like Johnny Boneck, throw temper tantrums to close the argument.

When I was a healthy, rational three year old, my mother held me on her lap as she read me a story. I moved my head from her left shoulder to the other side and back again and back again. I listened and squirmed. She warned me to sit still. I didn't obey. Finally she stopped reading and set me on the floor.

I lay on the floor and threw a great stimulus-response fit. I screamed and cried and kicked and waved my hands to get her to pick me up and resume the story. As I worked up a sweat, I happened to squint at Mom and Dad watching me from the kitchen table. Something was wrong. They didn't seem concerned at all! They actually seemed to be smiling. Then my mom got up from the table and stepped over the top of her screaming son and simply walked to the next room.

I didn't get it. After several minutes of exhaustive effort I stopped my rant. I got up and sat at the kitchen table. It was as if nothing had happened.

I didn't get my way, and my parents never said anything. But as a little boy I learned throwing temper tantrums doesn't always work.

Do we still throw tantrums when we don't get our way? Why didn't I get that promotion? Why is my church so dead? Why don't I get healed? Why don't I have enough money to buy a new car?

Matthew 5:13 says, "You are the salt of the earth; but if the salt loses its flavor, how shall it be seasoned? It is then good for nothing but to be thrown out and trampled underfoot by men." It is not about you, your wants, or your Christian ministry. It's about who you are.

How we live our Christian lives, how we interpret circumstances, how we view life itself is based on who we believe our Father is.

Our generation has seen a lot of what not to do and how not to live. However, love speaks truth and confronts us for our good.

Sometimes we Christians try to manipulate our Heavenly Father, too, wanting what we want, thinking we know best or that by begging, pleading, pouting, or screaming (praying) we will have our way.

Why doesn't our loving, sugar-daddy Father give us what we

want when we ask? After all, we're His children. Doesn't He care about us? Maybe He's not as loving as we thought.

Could it be that He knows more than we know, that He has our best interests in mind, that His ways are not our childish ways?

What can we do to bring our Father pleasure? We may need to repent. We may need to confess our sins and get back under the Father's love, protection, and provision.

In my younger years, actress Julie Andrews sang, "Just a spoonful of sugar helps the medicine go down." I've given some "sugary" personal examples in this book to help you to relate to me or the message more easily. But there is strong medicine needed also. The sugar doesn't heal; the medicine does.

Before we can be healed, we first must look at ourselves and recognize something's not right. Why don't I have the joy of the Lord? Why don't I know my purpose? Why do I feel others don't understand me? Why am I physically ill or upset so often?

It may be because we need medicine instead of sugar. Living a sugary Christian life isn't enough. Having gifts of the Spirit but not having a Godly character may be making you sick at heart. Hiding in the closet, avoiding the rest of the body of Christ, and calling yourself an intercessor may not be cutting it. Giving of your resources when you have a lot but not giving when you feel lack may not be working. Speaking in tongues to remind yourself you have a prayer language (as I did when I drank during my college days) may not be the right endgame.

Avoiding conflicts because you don't trust the Lord enough to bring reconciliation may not bring you peace. Judging pastors, those around you, your spouse, or others while you continue to read the Bible may interfere with your spiritual revelation and even your physical health. Keeping yourself ignorant of demonic attacks may not be allowing you to set captives or yourself free.

What about your former spouse and the resentment you

still carry that eats away at your peace and gives you stomach problems?

Oh, we need the Father's medicine to bring healing to our spirit, soul, and body.

How we live our Christian lives, how we interpret circumstances around us, how we view life itself are all based on who we believe our God is. Do we live like the "Egyptians" around us, in bondage to their idols and internet porn? Do we compromise our beliefs to better fit in with the rest of society?

He is the one who brings the cleansing fire. He is the one who has the only medicine that will heal us in every area of our lives. He still declares,

> *"If you diligently heed the voice of the Lord your God and do what is right in His sight, give ear to His commandments and keep all His statutes, I will put none of the diseases on you which I have brought on the Egyptians. For I am the Lord who heals you."* (Ex 15:26)

That is our Father.

The previous chapters revealed many of the loving aspects of our relational Heavenly Father. However, love involves more than giving us what we want and drawing us into a tender embrace in fear of losing our love. Oh no, love ultimately involves doing what is necessary to help us reach our mature potential, knowing it is for our good.

Sometimes love may not feel good to us at the moment. Psalm 30:5 says, "His anger is but for a moment, His favor is for life."

The prophet Ezekiel gave some strong prophetic words to the fellow Israelites who were now living in bondage in Babylon, taken from their homeland because of their own sins.

Ezekiel 36 reveals how the Heavenly Father's discipline works. The chapter opens by recounting that the other nations have now plundered the land of Israel. The previous chapter contained strong prophetic words against these evil nations. Our Father speaks through Ezekiel, saying, "Surely I have spoken in My burning jealousy against the rest of the nations and against all Edom, who gave My land to themselves as a possession, with wholehearted joy and spiteful minds, in order to plunder its open country." (Ezek 36:5) The Father's "burning jealousy" unleashed strong punishment for these nations. His fire is a burning, holy fire.

Later in the same chapter Ezekiel says to the fallen house of Israel:

> *Son of man, when the house of Israel dwelt in their own land, they defiled it by their own ways and deeds; to Me their way was like the uncleanness of a woman in her customary impurity. Therefore I poured out My fury on them for the blood they had shed on the land, and for their idols with which they had defiled it. So I scattered them among the nations, and they were dispersed throughout the countries; I judged them according to their ways and their deeds. When they came to the nations, wherever they went, they profaned My holy name—when they said of them, "These are the people of the Lord, and yet they have gone out of His land."*
> *But I had concern for My holy name, which the house of Israel had profaned among the nations wherever they went.*
> (Ezek 36:17-21)

Just as the Father punished the nations that had mocked and destroyed Israel, He also punished an extremely sinful chosen people. They shed sacrificial blood to other gods and set up false gods throughout the land, defiling it. He "judged them according to their ways and their deeds." They were guilty, guilty, guilty of making a mockery of the Father and His love. Why didn't He utterly destroy them or totally disown them? They had been so foul and brazenly unashamed of mocking, ignoring, and rejecting their Father.

Only a Father who knows the end from the beginning could look beyond such open disrespect. He has a solution. He is a wise and compassionate Father.

Ezekiel 36:24-29 continues the prophetic word:

I will take you from among the nations, gather you out of all countries, and bring you into your own land. Then I will sprinkle clean water on you, and you shall be clean; I will cleanse you from all your filthiness and from all your idols. I will give you a new heart and put a new spirit within you; I will take the heart of stone out of your flesh and give you a heart of flesh. I will put My Spirit within you and cause you to walk in My statutes, and you will keep My judgments and do them. Then you shall dwell in the land that I gave to your fathers; you shall be My people, and I will be your God. I will deliver you from all your uncleannesses.

All of mankind has sinned and come short of the glory of God (our Father), as Romans 3:23 says. In His great love He has to punish sin. In His great love He also provides a way out. The prophetic words in Ezekiel speak directly to the way out through Jesus Christ's own shed blood to cover our sin and unrighteousness and to send the Holy Spirit to lead us into all truth and Godly love.

The Father doesn't punish us because He likes to punish. He isn't mean and arbitrary. No, He is a loving Father. I learned this even as a little boy.

As I sat in the back seat of our 1949 Oldsmobile, I couldn't stop crying. Church had just ended. My father ordered me to go to the car and wait. I was going to get a spanking when we got home. Hence the tears.

I pictured how my father would take off his belt, double it, and then strike my behind. Although it didn't happen often, it made a stinging impression on my seat and on my memory.

We headed home, but I don't remember the conversations in the car. I do remember crying and trying to hold back sobs. We pulled into the driveway, and I got out of the car and went to my bedroom. I sat on the bed and waited for the closed bedroom door to open, knowing what it would mean.

The door opened, and in came my father. He slowly pulled off his belt. This was the moment of truth.

He told me to bend over. I obeyed. I got two swats from his belt and cried loudly the instant the first blow struck my behind. The truth is the sound was worse than the sting. Looking back, I know my dad realized I had suffered enough in the 20-minute car ride and that justice could be concluded with two light, promised swats.

I don't remember what I did to deserve my punishment but believe it was deserved. My relatives had given me the moniker "Johnny Don't." I was usually up to some kind of mischief.

The truth is "Foolishness is bound up in the heart of a child; the rod of correction will drive it far from him." (Prov 22:15) I was like all other children, and my father knew the remedy. After I got my "lickin'," my father stayed with me in the bedroom for a few minutes, and then we all went to the kitchen for our Sunday dinner, as noon-time meals were called in those days.

I never doubted my father's love. He wasn't arbitrary in his punishment and correction. I was privileged to grow up in a home where love was very real.

In reality my father had shown me mercy. He could have punished me severely. But this wasn't about taking out his anger on a disobedient child. It was about correcting the child for the child's benefit.

When God gave Moses the Ten Commandments on the mountain, He said, "I, the Lord your God, am a jealous God, visiting the iniquity of the fathers upon the children to the third and fourth generations of those who hate Me, but showing mercy to thousands, to those who love Me and keep My commandments." (Ex 20:5-6)

Though our Father will not ignore the sins of His children and will punish those who carry sinful intent, He will show mercy to those who love Him. He corrects us to mature us.

The Father's mercy is emphasized when He tells Moses how to build the tabernacle in the wilderness. The ark of the Testimony rests in the Holy of Holies. Very significantly, He tells of another special item in the holy of holies, the mercy seat. The Lord says,

> *You shall make a mercy seat of pure gold; two and a half cubits shall be its length and a cubit and a half its width. And you shall make two cherubim of gold; of hammered work you shall make them at the two ends of the mercy seat. Make one cherub at one end, and the other cherub at the other end; you shall make the cherubim at the two ends of it of one piece with the mercy seat. And the cherubim shall stretch out their wings above, covering the mercy seat with their wings, and they shall face one another; the faces of the cherubim shall be toward the mercy seat. You shall put the mercy seat on top of the ark, and in the ark you shall put the Testimony that I will give you. And there I will meet with you, and* **I will speak with you from above the mercy seat**, *from between the two cherubim which are on the ark of the Testimony, about everything which I will give you in commandment to the children of Israel.* (Ex 25:17-22, emphasis added)

In my earlier Christian days I would have expected God to speak to His people from above a judgment seat.

Instead He speaks from above the mercy seat.

What a picture this is of our loving Father. The reality is He has always wanted to show us mercy, not punishment. He is such a merciful Father, even when we don't deserve it.

James addresses the important distinction between judgment

and mercy. He says that to the person who lives outside the law, judgment will reign down on him. Those who intentionally choose their own way and make their own excuses and follow their own rules will live or die by their choices. But for us who know the love of the Father and want Him, to us James says, "Mercy triumphs over judgment." (James 2:13) We may not be perfect. We may sin again. But if our heart is after His heart, we can approach the "mercy seat." Will He ignore what we have done? No. He is righteous and will not ignore our actions. But He will provide a way back into relationship. It may even be by the "rod of correction."

The problem is that perpetual mischief and foolishness is not permanently driven out with a couple swats on the behind that my father administered to me.

When Adam and Eve sinned, foolishness entered the hearts of the Father's children. Rebellion became the modus operandi for mankind. A simple word search in the Old Testament of *rebellion* will prove the point.

Isaiah describes the results of mankind's rebellion.

Behold, the Lord's hand is not shortened, that it cannot save; neither his ear heavy, that it cannot hear: But your iniquities have separated between you and your God, and your sins have hid his face from you, that he will not hear. For your hands are defiled with blood, and your fingers with iniquity; your lips have spoken lies, your tongue hath muttered perverseness. None calleth for justice, nor any pleadeth for truth: they trust in vanity, and speak lies; they conceive mischief, and bring forth iniquity. (Is 59:1-4, KJV)

We separated ourselves from God our Father. He didn't separate himself from us. How severe must the rod of correction be for an individual or an entire nation acting in defiance to the Father, wanting to make themselves gods, choosing evil and sin continually?

People and nations didn't just sin a little. They sinned in ways we can't even comprehend. We get hints of their sins when we read how children were sacrificed to false gods and how travelers were sodomized when they came to such towns as Sodom and Gomorrah.

We see more glimpses of their sins when we read the prophets such as Ezekiel, Jeremiah, and Isaiah. God's chosen people created idols like those of the nations around them and worshiped wickedly and often in a sexually debauched manner at their altars. They mocked their Creator.

Only the Father's eternal plan of love and redemption prevented all of mankind from being wiped out for our wickedness.

But all was not lost. David, Enoch, Moses, Joshua, Caleb, and others looked to God the Father and didn't follow Satan's destructive ways which caused the "wrath of God" to be manifested at times.

When I was younger, I was very familiar with God's wrath. It seemed to appear throughout the Old Testament. The King James Version uses the term 151 times in the Old Testament alone. Not all the references are to God, but enough are that it seemed to be a dominant characteristic of the God of the Old Testament. Some people consider God, a God of wrath.

The King James and the New King James bibles imply we can also exhibit wrath. Ephesians 4:26 says, "Be angry, and do not sin: do not let the sun go down on your wrath." (NKJV)

Other versions of the Bible use the word *angry* instead of *wrath* in various places. For example, the NASB version says it this way. "Be angry, and yet do not sin; do not let the sun go down on your anger."

Wrath and *anger* seem to be interchangeable terms at times. It's interesting to note Paul did not tell the Ephesians not to be angry. He told them not to carry anger overnight. Get rid of it.

So, like our Father, we may get angry at times.

Jesus also expressed anger. Mark records an incident where Jesus met a man with a withered hand and wanted to heal him. However, it was on the Sabbath. Those in the synagogue watched Him closely "so that they might accuse Him." The story continues,

And He said to the man who had the withered hand, "Step forward." Then He said to them, "Is it lawful on the Sabbath to do good or to do evil, to save life or to kill?" But they kept silent. And when He had looked around at them with anger, being grieved by the hardness of their hearts, He said to the man, "Stretch out your hand." And he stretched it out, and his hand was restored as whole as the other. (Mark 3:3-5)

It shouldn't surprise us that our Father or Jesus shows anger. We who are made in His image carry similar emotions. How we handle those emotions demonstrates our spiritual condition. Our Father always acts from a foundation of righteousness and love.

The Father's anger or the more extreme term *wrath* is not generated from a selfish or power-hungry desire. He does not capriciously destroy people or nations. The people or nations determine their own fate. It starts at birth, as the verse in Proverbs about foolishness being bound up in the heart of a child indicates.

I can somewhat comprehend this on a personal scale, but when I try to fathom all the nations of the earth and the Father's oversight even of them, it is beyond my understanding.

The Apostle Paul recognized how unfathomable the Father's ways are as He exercises His work of ultimate love to draw us to Him. He says, "Oh, the depth of the riches both of the wisdom and knowledge of God! How unsearchable are His judgments and His ways past finding out!" (Rom 11:33) Whatever the Father does, He ultimately does it for our good, desiring to bring us back into relationship with Him.

Love is complicated. When we try to totally comprehend our Father's love and His actions, it is not possible to have a complete understanding. Rick Joyner shares some wise insight about Father God. Rick says,

> *It is difficult for some to understand how a God of love could allow all of the evil on the earth, much less bring the judgments, destruction, and wrath that are prophesied. This is confusing for those who try to interpret God through a human perspective, or their own opinions. As the Lord said through Isaiah: "For as the heavens are higher than the earth, so are My ways higher than your ways, and My thoughts than your thoughts" (Is 55:9).*

> *Some tend to think that God's emotions and feelings are just like ours, but they are not. Though they may have similarities, they are much higher than ours. When we are told that God is a jealous God, we can interpret as being like human jealousy, which is selfish and self-centered. However, God's jealousy is higher than ours—it is not so small hearted and selfish. His wrath, anger, and judgments are also not like ours—they are higher.[1]*

We can't fully comprehend the Father's Divine purposes or the height and depths of the Father's love. But we know He created us, wants to fellowship with us, and loves us.

When we see that our Father exhibits "wrath" or "anger," it can be easy to blame Him for everything that's wrong in our own lives. "He is mean." "He doesn't care about me." "He keeps punishing me because He is mad at me." "He doesn't want me to enjoy life." And so on.

---

1. https://www.morningstarministries.org/resources/word-week/2018/trusting-works-lord-book-revelation

Or, when we have suffered personal loss or have lost our job or have had a breakdown in our family, we can say, "Where is this loving God? He doesn't care about me."

If you lived with a father who was mean, thoughtless, abusive, or neglectful, it can be hard to see that God our Father is different. When we read about "God's wrath" in the Old Testament, it can be easy to think our Heavenly Father is no different from our earthly father. And that is exactly what Satan wants us to think.

One of the great dilemmas in child rearing is how to properly demonstrate to the child that there are consequences for behavior. My father swatted my behind in a stinging way, and I got the point.

On a larger scale, lack of correction leads to lawlessness. Some parents may be afraid to hurt their child's self-image by applying firm correction, instead simply calling a "time out" to let their little cherub know they shouldn't do that. Some of us might even say that is simply applying "grace" as God the Father has also shown.

Hebrews reveals a different stance, however. We realize that if our Father had not had grace for mankind in our sinful, shameful, rebellious condition, we would all be lost. He has great grace. But He is also a righteousness judge who applies firm correction when needed.

Hebrews 10:30-31 says,

"The Lord will judge his people." It is a dreadful thing to fall into the hands of the living God.

Our Father's ways are much higher than our ways. But I know He has our best in mind, even when He corrects us.

The very beginning of the Father's autobiography reveals that our Father is a creator who wants a loving relationship with us Adams and Eves. He gives them everything and communes with them. Sadly, they listen to Satan and rebel against the Father's directions. As the autobiography continues, we see how the Father reaches specific people and even calls forth a chosen nation to rebuild the trust and love. During all this time we read how evil and perverted and untrusting so many of us humans are.

The autobiography continues. In His extraordinary mercy, He sends His only begotten Son to be a substitute for our sins, not wanting any of us to perish but to instead have eternal life with Him, as John 3:16 says.

And the Father's story continues, revealing through the apostles some of the great benefits of being sons and daughters of such a loving Father.

His autobiography concludes prophetically, telling us of our glorious future with Him and the destruction of Satan who interfered with the Father's children in the Garden of Eden and throughout history.

PART TWO:
CARRYING THE
FATHER'S FIRE

Living Out Our Kingdom Identity

"I and My Father are one." (Jn 10:30)

We know who our Father is and feel His love. We know He has a Kingdom. We are sons and daughters of our Heavenly Father, as the first part of this book proclaimed. From that revelation and understanding, we grow in our Kingdom identity and walk a new path.

Sadly, many Christians do not really understand their spiritual identity.

Very recently I sat in church listening to yet another request for us to give a generous offering. Usually I can handle requests for offerings pretty well, but something was different this time.

As part of the speaker's plea, he quoted Barna Group findings, stating that less than 10% of all those who call themselves Christians tithe and about 25% of Charismatic/Pentecostal Christians tithe. "Imagine," he continued, "what impact the church could have around the world if all Spirit-filled Christians tithed?"

I imagine we could do great things, and that would be wonderful. But something else was stirring in me.

He wasn't trying to manipulate us. I was stirred up inside

because it was abundantly clear that we Spirit-filled Christians don't really know who we are. Of the 25% of Spirit-filled Christians, I imagine some tithe because they believe it's the right thing to do, some give because they feel it's their Christian responsibility, some give because they follow Christian "laws."

I wonder, however, how many of the 25% tithe because they know who they are as sons and daughters of the Father.

In the book of Acts Spirit-filled Christians were those who turned the world upside down. Now we're lucky if we can cough up a good offering. Why aren't people running to us like they ran to Jesus, the Son of the Father? Maybe it's because we only carry a title rather than living in our identity as a son or daughter of the Father the way Jesus did.

We are to have more than a "Spirit-filled Christian" title. If our Father owns the cattle on a thousand hills and we have access to all that, should we quibble about whether or not we should tithe?

Are we Spirit-filled Christians the prodigal from Jesus' story who squanders the great inheritance his father has given him? Yet the father waits, looking to the horizon for a glimpse of his confused, destitute child to return to him.

The way Jesus tells the story, the prodigal returns and the father throws him a party, celebrating his return. What Jesus doesn't mention is that after the prodigal repents, he most likely goes to his bedroom and cries, overcome by his father's great love. He probably tears off his dirty garments and takes a cleansing shower to remove the smell of the pig farm from his body. He probably opens the closet door and puts on the clothes that reflect he is a son of this loving father who, though he owns everything, allows his children to choose for themselves whether or not to live in his love in his kingdom.

The prodigal steps back into his identity.

Christ came to earth to reconcile us to the Father, not to make us Spirit-filled Christians whose goal is to learn more about how to function in the gifts. His message was about the Kingdom of His Father and showing us how to communicate with Him and be reunited with His great love. He wants us to "seek the Kingdom" above all things, living as sons and daughters of our Father. (Matt 6:33)

Our elder brother, Jesus, demonstrates what being a son or daughter of the Heavenly Father looks like. He heals the sick, casts out demons, sets the captives free. He is also misunderstood and judged and condemned by those who want religion more than relationship.

The early church understands the message. They do what Jesus did and "turned the world upside down." That's because they know who they are. They don't have a title. Others give them the title as Christians to identify this unique Kingdom-living group.

As I demonstrated in the first part of this book, any reading of the epistles will show you that the writers know the Father and not just a message about Jesus, the Holy Spirit, and spiritual gifts.

Paul begins most of his epistles by recognizing the Father. For example, he opens his letter to the Ephesians, saying,

Grace to you and peace from God our Father and the Lord Jesus Christ. Blessed be the God and Father of our Lord Jesus Christ, who has blessed us with every spiritual blessing in the heavenly places in Christ. (Eph 1:2-3)

The God of creation is our grace-giving and peace-fulfilling Father. He's the Father of our Lord Jesus Christ, as well. He's not just a title. He is our Father. He's not just the God of the Old Testament as the Jews knew Him and how some Christians still may think of Him. He IS our Father. Our Father. Our loving and forgiving Father.

In Jeremiah 3 the Father speaks to the children He has created. They rejected Him, much like the New Testament prodigal does. They wanted their own way and had hard hearts. They wanted to live religious lives on their own terms, preferring other relationships to the relationship with the One who had created them and wanted to provide for them. No wonder they were afraid of Him when He and Moses met on the mountain. Now in the land of Promise they didn't know Him or want Him. He was a threat to their religious ways. They would rather worship the work of their own hands. (Jer 1:16) They wanted to have religion on their own terms, rejecting relationship.

God the Father sees this, and still He beckons to His children:

How gladly would I treat you like my children
and give you a pleasant land,
the most beautiful inheritance of any nation.
I thought you would call me 'Father'
and not turn away from following me. (Jer 3:19, NIV)

It is so easy for us, even as Spirit-filled Christians, to miss our true identity as sons and daughters of the Father, living from His Kingdom perspective. He gives us gifts, and we focus on them rather than on Him. We try to figure out how to use a particular gift and get better at perfecting its use. But if we don't know who we are as a son or daughter, we won't fully understand the Father's purpose for the gift.

Our Father knows all this. He is calling us back to Himself.

In His next fiery move He's going to clean us up and purge us so we can live a Kingdom identity that will turn our present world upside down. He's coming to set us on fire again, even at our age. Watch out for His cleansing fire, turning us to gold, as Revelation 3:18 says. His fire is coming, and we will be changed from religious titles to relationship. We will cast off our dirty religious garments and wear His covering.

Until a decade ago when the Father hugged me, I had never

identified with the personal love the Father has for us. Since then it has been the joy of my life.

Obvious scriptures such as **John 3:16** took on added significance to me:

God so loved the world that He gave his only begotten Son, that whoever believes in Him should not perish but have everlasting life.

- God the Father loves us.
- He made a personal sacrifice to bring us back to His arms.
- I will have an eternal relationship with the Father. I am His son.

Romans took on an entirely personal understanding.

For as many as are led by the Spirit of (the Father), these are **sons of (the Father)**. *For you did not receive the spirit of bondage again to fear, but you received the Spirit of adoption by whom we cry out,* **"Abba, Father**.*" The Spirit Himself bears witness with our spirit that we are* **children of (the Father)**, *and if children, then* **heirs—heirs of (the Father)** *and joint heirs with Christ.* (Rom 8:14-16)

I had read Romans 8 probably about 50 times over the years. For the first time I understood sonship.

And He removed the bondage. He set this captive soldier free.

In 2005 I was on a business trip to Anchorage, Alaska. I heard MorningStar Ministries was holding a prophetic training seminar in Wasilla the same weekend I was there. I decided to stay over and learn more about the prophetic. My wife and I had attended several conferences at MorningStar Ministries and were hungry for more. During the prophetic training I practiced how to hear from the Holy Spirit. I surprised myself, discovering how the Holy Spirit really wants to work through me. As a matter of fact, I felt I was getting pretty good.

After a full day's training, I went to my hotel room in Wasilla, feeling pretty pleased with the day's activities. Although I was not used to having prophetic dreams, that night I had a dream that brought me to a new reality.

I dreamed I was in a beautiful castle. Everything was white and pure. I looked around and noticed the beautiful white draperies on the windows were largely transparent, allowing me to peer through them. I went to the window. Then I saw them. The soldiers of the King. They were regal and totally armed and shining white, riding beautiful white steeds, and heading out to battle.

But here I was inside the castle looking out. Then I woke up.

I realized I wasn't white and pure. I wasn't ready for the battle. Many tears stained my pillow that night as I wept before the Lord, asking forgiveness for all my sins and impure ways of living, even as a Spirit-filled Christian who was growing in the prophetic. It was part of the fire of God exposing the dross in my life to purify me.

Much has happened in my life since then. A few months ago I had another dream. I was on an upward path. I knew the way. I looked ahead and saw a castle in the distance. This wasn't just any castle. I knew this was the Father's house and I was on my way toward it as a son of the Father.

I could never be doing what I am doing today if I hadn't discovered my real identity. Being a nice Spirit-filled person wasn't enough. Working for Jesus wasn't sufficient. The Father wants more.

He wants a personal relationship with me. He wants me to know who I really am. Everything else will grow from that. Now I want to call God by His love name, Father.

One of the outcomes of having my identity is that I no longer take offense or become easily offended by others. The years I carried a spiritual wound I could be offended by what someone said or by my perception of what they did or meant or perhaps thought of me. I was judging based on my broken-heart experiences.

Do I still get angry at time? Yes. Do I falsely judge some people at times? Yes. But I notice that it happens much, much less often than when I was wounded. I am able to quickly forgive. My relationship with the Father is more important than what others say or think. Oh, the beauty of having an unoffendable heart!

To live in our true God-created identity, we have to get over ourselves. We are not little gods. The world does not revolve around our needs and desires (even our "spiritual" desires). It doesn't revolve around our children either.

The Father desires intimacy with each one of us. Everything we do is based on that. Jesus said, "I and My Father are one." (Jn 10:30) We can say the same thing as we allow His love to overtake our lives.

My purpose and passion and very existence come from who I am, from my identity as a son of the Father of love, with my wounds healed.

His love is the ultimate answer for identity.

The working for Him or trying to please Him in my own efforts or from what I thought He required of a good Christian is gone.

It was that way for Paul. He had his identity. Philippians 3:3-11 gives us a good example:

For we are the circumcision, who worship God in the Spirit, rejoice in Christ Jesus, and have no confidence in the flesh, though I also might have confidence in the flesh. If anyone else thinks he may have confidence in the flesh, I more so: circumcised the eighth day, of the stock of Israel, of the tribe of Benjamin, a Hebrew of the Hebrews; concerning the law, a Pharisee; concerning zeal, persecuting the church; concerning the righteousness which is in the law, blameless.

But *what things were gain to me, these I have counted loss for Christ. Yet indeed I also count all things loss for the excellence of the knowledge of Christ Jesus my Lord, for whom I have suffered the loss of all things, and count them as rubbish, that I may gain Christ and be found in Him, not having my own righteousness, which is from the law, but that which is through faith in Christ,* **the righteousness which is from (the Father) by faith***; that I may know Him and the power of His resurrection, and the fellowship of His sufferings, being conformed to His death, if, by any means, I may attain to the resurrection from the dead.*

In Philippians 3:3 he says real believers don't have any confidence in the flesh.

In verses 4-6, he mentions his fleshly things:

If anyone else thinks he may have confidence in the flesh, I more so: circumcised the eighth day, of the stock of Israel, of the tribe of Benjamin, a Hebrew of the Hebrews; concerning the law, a Pharisee; concerning zeal, persecuting the church; concerning the righteousness which is in the law, blameless.

He recites his religious credentials first, just as we can recite our certificates of accomplishment in Christian courses, our seminary training, etc. He says real believers don't have any confidence in these things.

Verses 7-9 tell us he put away religious works, ways of trying to please the Father. And he tells us his goal in life--that I may gain Christ and be found in Him. It reads:

But what things were gain to me, these I have counted loss for Christ. Yet indeed I also count all things loss for the excellence of the knowledge of Christ Jesus my Lord, for whom I have suffered the loss of all things, and count them as rubbish, that I may gain Christ and be found in Him, not having my own righteousness, which is from the law, but that which is through faith in Christ, the righteousness which is from God (the Father) by faith.

How much are we willing to give up?

Notice how the Father is also in the mix. It is the Father who sets this plan in motion in Paul and all Christians. We want to know our Father. We want to be found in Christ. We want to live that identity.

Then, and only then, our purpose flows.

We can tell we are getting our priorities straight when striving and anxiety leave, no matter what. Paul puts it this way in Philippians 4:6-7:

Be anxious for nothing, but in everything by prayer and supplication with thanksgiving let your requests be made known to (the Father). And (the Father's) peace, which surpasses all comprehension, will guard your hearts and your minds in Christ Jesus. (Phil 4:6-7)

Both heart and mind are guarded. It is more than mental reasoning.

When you know who you are, anointing and power are present. You have a vocation, but the vocation isn't who you are. It is what you do. You carry who you are into the vocation.

You take yourself with you wherever you move. I did.

When you know who you are, you can live in purpose in different circumstances and not have the circumstances dominate your decision process. Abraham, Paul, Peter, John, David, and many others in the Bible did this.

Circumstances can crush you if you are running under your own religious steam. I know a man in his 40s who is a Christian. He wants to make good decisions for himself and his family. He is very moral. He also applies Christian rules to his circumstances and to his family. However, he operates from his mental reasoning of Godly principles rather than from the mind of Christ. In other words, he thinks religiously rather than spiritually. Thus, he has broken relationships around him because he becomes the judge of others' actions.

The Galatian church had the same problem when some of them wanted to go back to following the law of the Old Covenant. This fine Christian man who is saved has not discovered his true identity. The Apostle Paul tells the Roman Christians they are to be transformed by the renewing of their minds. (Rom 12:2) Then they will be able to discern spiritually.

The bottom line is we don't just accept Jesus into our hearts. We surrender our entire being (spirit, soul, and body) to Him. We give up our ways, even our good ways, of thinking to allow the Holy Spirit to guide our thoughts and actions. The Father is spiritual. We as sons and daughters are also to live in the Spirit.

When I was hurt in the church, I wanted others to recognize and affirm me. I wanted an identity. Wanting to have people recognize us and maybe the gifts we have only leads to a false religious identity. It is a battle at times for us to take ourselves off the throne of our lives. When we do, however, real purpose begins. We step outside our own ways of thinking and can live out two great commandments.

Jesus tells us their proper sequence:

Then one of the scribes came, and having heard them reasoning together, perceiving that He had answered them well, asked Him, "Which is the first commandment of all?"

Jesus answered him, "The first of all the commandments is: 'Hear, O Israel, the Lord our God, the Lord is one. **And you shall love the Lord your God with all your heart, with all your soul, with all your mind, and with all your strength.** *' This is the first commandment. And the* **second,** *like it, is this:* **'You shall love your neighbor as yourself.'** *There is no other commandment greater than these." (*Mark 12:28-31)

Two commandments--love the Lord your God (our Father) with your entire being and love your neighbor as yourself. These two commandments are as valid today as when Jesus spoke them. What is holding you back from doing this?

- Are you mad at God because of something that happened to you?
- Do you have a fear of what others will think of you?
- Do you desire acceptance in order to feel complete?
- Do you judge God because life isn't the way you want it?
- Do you blame Him for the death of someone close to you?
- Does a hurt or abuse from your past keep you trapped?
- Do you feel judged by others because you are a different skin color or divorced or not well off, etc., and thus can't love others?

Surrender yourself. A love relationship with the Father is the first thing. Then you can be an evangelist if you want or love those around you or go on speaking tours (if, indeed, that is really what the Father is leading you to).

Romans 8:28-9 gives another example of the sequence of identity and then purpose. It says,

CARRYING THE FATHER'S FIRE

And we know that all things work together for good to those who love God (our identity is a love relationship with the Father)*, to those who are the called according to His purpose* (then we have purpose)*. For whom He foreknew, He also predestined to be conformed to the image of His Son, that He might be the firstborn among many brethren.*

We love the Father, connecting in identity. Then we have purpose. Furthermore, we will take on the image of the Father's beloved Son, Jesus.

Our culture and present generation impact how the Father will use us. However, He has put our future into our individual spiritual makeups and knows where we can best be used. The goal isn't to be best used, although that might feel wonderful. The main thing is to know who we are based on how the Father created us.

A Millennial friend of mine was hurt in her childhood years, living in a dysfunctional family. As a result, she longed for acceptance but was insecure. She and her husband became pastors in a church plant, and they were wounded there, too, when some other young leaders turned on them.

But they hungered for real love, and the Father showed up in their lives and healed them. Though an earthly father had failed her and even friends had failed her, she chose to trust her Heavenly Father. She pushed through the lie of insecurity that Satan had planted in her heart to find the Truth.

Now she proclaims herself a warrior. She learned how to overcome the enemy of her soul and looks to do battle with him wherever she goes. She and her husband are impacting many people around them because they cast off Satan's lies and allowed the love of the Father to give them identity, replacing the lies with His love in their hearts.

When Satan tries to speak false insecurity to her, she simply proclaims that she is accepted in the Beloved. It truly is a faith walk.

There are two voices wanting to catch our attention and impact our heart. One voice is the Holy Spirit. The other voice is Satan. We must always recognize the voice.

Does the voice encourage you and make you stronger? Does it make you fall more in love with Jesus? Does it bring peace to your circumstances? Does it help you look outside your own circumstances to desire healing for those who don't know the voice? Does it help your personal relationships become stronger? Well, that voice is from above, from the Father of lights.

The other voice makes you feel insecure. It makes you doubt yourself, your abilities, and others. It says you are a failure. It says your sinful habits can never be removed. It says others are saying bad things about you. It tells you that you will never fit in. It says you have no hope for a good future. It speaks that the illness you carry can never be made better. It says your children will never return to the Lord. It tells you that you have to work harder for Jesus in order to be accepted. It discourages and depresses you and keeps you from living an active life of love.

Really, it's not hard to recognize which voice you are hearing. The question is, "What will you do when you hear the wrong voice?" We will address this question in depth in the next chapter because identity and inner healing go together.

When we live in our identity as sons and daughters of the Father, we know His voice and reject the enemy's lies. We start seeing from the Father's perspective instead of our own religious view. We become able to understand what is of real and lasting worth instead of living in vanity.

So, how do we reconnect with the Father? For me the Father had to actually give me a physical hug. I didn't have those around me who had discernment about spiritual wounds. Ask the Father to connect you with others who are after His heart.

The body of Christ is made up of individual interconnected members. If you do not connect with other believers, your identity will be incomplete; some of your healing may not happen. We are to pray for each other that we might be healed. Ask the Father to connect you with some others.

There are some other ways I want to mention also. It begins with getting back to basics.

As a Christian in a me-centered society and in me-centered churches, break away from the pack. Let your life be all about loving the Father and Jesus our Savior. Don't get your affirmation from others or from Christian work; receive it from the Father.

Before you read the Bible, ask the Holy Spirit to reveal the Father's intent in the Scripture you are reading. Stop looking for solutions to your problems and instead read the Word to have Him reveal who He is and what He's about. When you have a revelation of His love, your problems either diminish or are seen in a new light.

Before you pray, simply sit and say, "Father, you have permission to speak to me. I want to know Your voice." Have a journal or something to capture what you hear.

You might also want to write down a request (another way to pray) that you speak to the Father. It could be something like the following:

Father, I want you in my life as my true Father. I want to know the real God from the false gods. Show me my false worship of things, recognition, and achievements that I make more important than You.

Forgive me, Father, for judging You and blaming You for what went wrong in my past. I know You didn't want anything bad to happen to me but that Satan did. I repent and will not allow Satan's destructive acts and plans to control my real identity anymore.

Father, expose the lies I've listened to. I give them to you and ask the blood of Jesus Christ to cleanse my heart and mind.

Father, I give you my ideas, plans, and actions. Raise me up as a Kingdom warrior, restoring Your Kingdom wherever I go.

I know, Father, that not everything is the way I want it. That's o.k. I just want my life to be the way You want it. I declare I will revel in Your love. I have my identity in You.

50+ers may feel the glory years are past. You might have grown up in the Jesus movement or during the Charismatic Movement, seeing miracles and lives changed. But now the years have taken their toll. Is there really a fiery God future, where His presence and His people restore the beauty of relationship?

Our Father says, "Yes."

We are a prophetic picture of the latter temple Haggai talks about. Many Jews returned to Jerusalem after 70 years of bondage. They suffered much and now were being called to once again build the temple. They were weary, however, and wanted to settle down in the place they once loved. They built themselves retirement homes. But they were being called to more. They were to restore.

Haggai speaks:

For thus says the Lord of hosts: "Once more (it is a little while) I will shake heaven and earth, the sea and dry land; and I will shake all nations, and they shall come to the Desire of All Nations, and I will fill this temple with glory," says the Lord of hosts. "The silver is Mine, and the gold is Mine," says the Lord of hosts. "The glory of this latter temple shall be greater than the former," says the Lord of hosts. "And in this place I will give peace," says the Lord of hosts." (Hag 2:6-9)

The Father is calling them to once again build His temple. He wants them to take burned stones and fashion them into a place for His glory to dwell.

We may have seen our personal temple crushed and cast down. We may feel like we're trampled on, almost like we've been invaded. We may feel powerless and ruled by foreign forces.

But God our Father is saying to us, "Build My temple!" His peace is going to abide in us. The fiery cleansing is purifying us, letting us know who we really are. We are His temple.

As His temple, we want to be clean inside and out. The next chapter addresses how that is possible.

Cleansing Our Temple

When evening had come, they brought to Him many who were demon-possessed. And He cast out the spirits with a word. (Matt 8:16)

Discovering our identity as a son or daughter of the Heavenly Father does not mean we are automatically whole spirit, soul, and body. Instead it gives us the ability to listen to His voice instead of other voices that would try to destroy our lives and our loves.

When we know our Father, we recognize that we come under His authority and can overcome the evil one, Satan, who has tried to keep us in a false identity or in a weakened Christian state.

Satan and his imps are pests. Let me use a homey example to paint a picture for you.

Sandy and I sat in our 3-year-old home, watching TV and relaxing. We felt so comfortable in the home we had built. We didn't know we had been invaded.

Married three and a half years earlier, we both felt secure in each other's love and were overwhelmed at times at how the Father had blessed us. I had made the transition from being a widower to being happily married. For Sandy it meant having a husband again after 26 years of suffering from divorce and having to raise and provide for three young children. We both wanted to start our lives together in a fresh way in new surroundings.

Sandy and I made many decisions initially to create the home of our dreams, with extra space for our five children and nine grandchildren to stay when they visited. Sandy continued improving the house, adding the right window coverings, getting some different furniture to add to the décor, and much more. We felt we were finally settled in.

Then we heard it.

It was a gnawing sound coming from the kitchen area. We looked at each other, perplexed. It didn't take us long to realize a mouse was on the loose. We should have recognized the signs earlier. One day after coming home from a trip, I went into the guest bathroom and saw what looked like crumpled up paper or cloth fragments on the floor. Could this be something that came from the air vent above? I didn't think so. Could the person who was housesitting for us have left this little mess? Well, maybe. But I still had my doubts.

The next thing we discovered was that the sponges in the small foldout drawer in front of the kitchen sink were half destroyed. At this point I thought, "Maybe we have some palmetto bugs under the sink." Those pesky bugs can get mighty large in the South. But I should have known better.

When we heard the gnawing sound coming from the wall, we knew our sanctuary had an unwanted guest. Several mousetraps later and a visit from an exterminator handled the pest. But that wasn't the end of the story. In the coming days we discovered just how much the critter had ruled at our house.

Sandy went to the upper drawer in a cabinet in my office to get a birthday card. She kept many special occasion cards there so she wouldn't have to scramble when there was a birthday or some other special event. Oh, no. The mouse had been there. The edges were gnawed off many of the cards, rendering them useless. That mouse had attacked our tokens of love to others.

An equally disturbing discovery occurred when Sandy went into a drawer in her office that held special family pictures from the past. Evidently mice like photographic chemicals. The little pest was attacking our family history and memories. How that mouse could get into those drawers baffled us.

We should have expected it, I suppose. After all, the furry little thing had completely gnawed its way around the drain pipe under the kitchen sink and had taken up residence there for a time.

When Sandy reached for a scarf from the top of our bedroom closet and mouse dropping also came down, we realized we had been living with an invader for a long time and didn't recognize it.

I believe the mouse invasion is very similar to how the enemy of our souls can operate in our lives if we are not aware.

Recently I was with some 50+ers at a prayer time. I asked one of the ladies how she was doing. I knew she had a ministry to others in another country. She often talked about them and what the Lord was doing in their lives. I said to her, "How are you doing personally, not your ministry. I just want to know how you're doing."

She then shared a very recent powerful personal breakthrough over a previously unrecognized issue that had thrived in her spiritual house for nine years. She had been hurt in a bad marriage relationship about a decade earlier. Ever since the divorce she had unreasonable fear manifesting itself in her life. The fear would pop up at the most inopportune times (just like that little mouse), hurting her relationships and fostering distrust even though she really loved the Lord and ministered to others. It was Satan's little rodent sneaking into her temple, creating hidden havoc.

She knew she wasn't personally happy but didn't know what was wrong. Finally, she went for some help from members of our spiritual healing teams at MorningStar. They didn't meet to counsel her or give her advice. Instead they invited the Holy Spirit to reveal the source of her unhappiness. During the course of their time together the Holy Spirit revealed to her the source. She saw that a spirit of fear had attacked her ever since her divorce. An imp from hell had taken advantage of access through an open wound and made a nest, keeping her from living in joy and trust. She had never realized why she carried these unreasonable fears.

The ministry teams prayed with her and cast out the spirit of fear, replacing the wound with the healing of the Holy Spirit.

When she told us the story, she was now smiling. The spiritual rodent had been exterminated and her spiritual house was in order. It could no longer attack her desire to love and trust others. It couldn't nibble away at pictures of her true identity. She was now living in peace. And she realized she could now minister to others more powerfully because she had experienced the Father's healing love and restoration for His precious daughter.

John 10:10 encapsulates the eternal battle being waged over each of our lives. Jesus explains it, saying,

The thief does not come except to steal, and to kill, and to destroy. I have come that they may have life, and that they may have it more abundantly.

Satan, that great thief, tries to steal our happiness, rob us of our identity, and even kill us. He is not visible in his attacks on our lives. He moves covertly, in the shadows. We cannot see him with our natural eyes, though we may experience his actions or see the results of his hideous activities in others' lives. Much of the church is blind to his activities, not recognizing that there are two sides in a battle. If you do not recognize the enemy, you cannot defeat him.

When Jesus came to free us and give us life, He freed us from the enemy's prison and restored the lives that Satan was in the process of destroying. We know that Jesus promised to give us life, abundant life. The Holy Spirit will shine a healing light on the source of hurts, anxieties, and shame when we give Him the chance. It may take cleansing help from some spiritually mature people to stand with us, but Satan's attempted power to control can and will be broken.

Many, many Christians carry wounds from various circumstances. Then Satan, who wants to defeat us, sends an imp of hell to establish a stronghold in that broken area.

If the enemy's stronghold on your soul isn't removed, your view of the Father, yourself, and of others is skewed, as was the case with me for decades. You see things through the prism of your wound.

Good soldiers can be taken captive after they're already in the army. I was a good soldier who was filled with the Holy Spirit and wanted to serve the Lord. But I was taken captive to a wound.

We forget we are in spiritual warfare always. Paul declares,

For the weapons of our warfare are not carnal but mighty in God for pulling down strongholds. (2 Cor 10:4)

And in the letter to the Ephesians he writes,

Finally, my brethren, be strong in the Lord and in the power of His might. Put on the whole armor of God, that you may be able to stand against the wiles of the devil. For we do not wrestle against flesh and blood, but against principalities, against powers, against the rulers of the darkness of this age, against spiritual hosts of wickedness in the heavenly places. Therefore take up the whole armor of God, that you may be able to withstand in the evil day, and having done all, to stand. (Eph 6:10-13)

We need spiritual armor because we are in a battle. Our enemy is our enemy whether we want to fight or not. We can be captured or overrun or be under his dominion when we are not aware that we are warriors and soldiers of the cross.

We can't get bogged down in past wounds, offense, or disappointments that hinder us from moving ahead.

When we are wounded, Satan keeps feeding us lies and oppresses us to keep us from entering fully into the Kingdom love of the Father.

When we are wounded, the wound dominates--

- It helps shape our personality.
- Our personal choices lead to disappointment instead of contentment and joy.
- The wound forms our outlook. We see everything through the prism of our wound and make our decisions in such a way that the wound is protected.
- We may divorce ourselves from intimate relationship--with the Father and others. We don't quite know how to relate.
- We put on masks, although we may not know it, so others won't see us as struggling to find purpose or definition to our lives.
- We judge others because the wound distorts our perspective. We don't fit in churches.
- We may carry shame, guilt, and fear that the wound keeps revealing.
- Religious activity replaces spiritual life. I tried to do many Christian things when I was wounded, but there was no anointing on them. Kingdom life is totally different from the solo religious life.

When I carried a wound, I wanted to fit in but couldn't. I walked in my own solo identity. I knew Jesus and was filled with the Holy Spirit, but my soul was not cleaned out. I needed a house cleaning, a personal temple cleansing.

It wasn't that I was harboring a secret sin, although this can be the issue for some Christians. It was that something in life happened to me. In reality I was violated in my soul and carried the violation as a wound. It was spiritual abuse. Then an imp of hell established a stronghold, distorting truth and relationship.

You can be violated in many, many different ways. It could be a divorce. It could be a sexual attack, it could be verbal abuse, it could be an atmosphere of lack, it could be being misjudged, etc., etc. Christ has come to set the captives free. The Father loves us; He doesn't condemn us.

You may have done some things that keep you feeling condemnation. The Father wants to cleanse that in your life also.

Satan wants us to live in our old-man nature. The Father wants us to be free spirit, soul, and body. The Father wants us to live in our new, true identity.

Since the Father healed me, I have noticed that people can be prophetic, operate in spiritual gifts, even heal people, and still have wounds. Actually some of these gifts may allow them to cover up the issues they carry.

I think some of us can be like the prodigal son who received the inheritance from the father. He had his gift. But he was outside the father's love and protection. The Father wants us to operate under His authority and in His love in His Kingdom!

Many Christian men think that lust is just something we have to put up with because of our testosterone levels. But the lust may have its roots from abandonment at a young age, rejection from the opposite sex during key teenage years, pornography, or something else.

Some pastors and many of the rest of us can operate with a solo mentality, creating false identities because they have never dealt with the soul wounds they suffered in the past. It could be a father who forced them to be perfect. It could be guilt from a past sexual encounter. It could be almost anything.

Religion is Satan's mask for a pretend spirituality.

The Kingdom is family! Religion is solo. Are you separated and solo? You may have a wound the Father wants to heal. If you can't join with others in Kingdom life and love, something is missing or wrong.

There's a difference between having been wounded and still carrying a wound. Christians are going to suffer wounds on the battlefield. The question is, "Is the wound healed?" Bob Jones said Christians could have scars. It shows they were battling but that the wounds are healed and not still festering.

As I look back on my own experience, the wound owned me and kept me feeling like an orphan, not being able to fit in. We feel like foster children, even in church.

To determine your position in the family of the Kingdom of God, you can answer two questions:

- Who fathers you? You must have a love relationship with the Father.
- Who are you joined with? Are you alone or possibly with others who are wounded? Or, are you operating as part of the Kingdom family?

When Jesus visited His hometown of Nazareth, he went to a synagogue and read portions of Isaiah 61 and proclaimed that the verses applied to Him. Two things He was anointed to do were to proclaim liberty to the captives and to set at liberty those who are oppressed. (Is 61:1)

We too are called to bring liberty to those who are "captive"--to addictions and lusts and false beliefs that Satan has placed in their lives. Our Father is calling us to set those captives free, to deliver them from their bondage. We 50+ers, walking in our identity, go to battle against Satan and his horde to set the captives around us free.

We are also called to lead any who are "oppressed" into liberty. Satan wants to crush any believer who is down. He some-times uses people to do this. He sometimes uses circumstances. He sometimes uses lying spirits to bring discouragement.

Delivering people from bondage and bringing liberty to the oppressed require healing of the soul. We are called to bring deliverance. We have the authority to cast out oppressing spirits that have tormented believers and non-believers alike.

The church often just deals with the spirit for salvation and then uses the mind to counsel people. The Father wants much more. His fire is coming to cleanse and purify us. He wants a place to dwell. We are to be cleaned up and cleaned out as the temple of the Holy Spirit.

We should spiritually look like the original physical temple. King David had prepared the way for his son Solomon to build it. And Solomon was up to the task. Chapters two through seven of Second Chronicles record how the temple was built. When it was completed, Solomon dedicated it and prayed.

When Solomon had finished praying, fire came down from heaven and consumed the burnt offering and the sacrifices; and the glory of the Lord filled the temple. And the priests could not enter the house of the Lord, because the glory of the Lord had filled the Lord's house. When all the children of Israel saw how the fire came down, and the glory of the Lord on the temple, they bowed their faces to the ground on the pavement, and worshiped and praised the Lord, saying:

"For He is good,

For His mercy endures forever." (2 Chron 7:1-3)

The Father's fire is coming to us, too. His glory is going to fill our personal temple. It will be cleansed and pure, a dwelling place for our Holy Father.

Jesus understood the importance of having a pure temple.

John 2:13-17 records that right after Jesus performs His first miracle of turning the water into wine, manifesting His glory (His Godness), He goes to Jerusalem at the time of Passover and enters the temple--

Now the Passover of the Jews was at hand, and Jesus went up to Jerusalem. And He found in the temple those who sold oxen and sheep and doves, and the money changers doing business. When He had made a whip of cords, He drove them all out of the temple, with the sheep and the oxen, and poured out the changers' money and overturned the tables. And He said to those who sold doves, "Take these things away! Do not make My Father's house a house of merchandise!" Then His disciples remembered that it was written, "Zeal for Your house has eaten Me up."

Matthew 21:12-14 says it this way:

Then Jesus went into the temple of God and drove out all those who bought and sold in the temple, and overturned the tables of the money changers and the seats of those who sold doves. And He said to them, "It is written, 'My house shall be called a house of prayer,' but you have made it a 'den of thieves.' "

Then the blind and the lame came to Him in the temple, and He healed them.

Jesus wanted a dwelling place for the Father. He wanted the temple cleansed to become a house of prayer, a place of communion and communication with the Father, a place where people are healed. Why? Because that's what He wants for us. He wasn't just performing spring cleaning. It was a prophetic symbol for what we are to look like.

Paul tells the Corinthians in 1 Cor. 3:16-17:

Do you not know that you are the temple of God and that the Spirit of God dwells in you? If anyone defiles the temple of God, God will destroy him. For the temple of God is holy, which temple you are.

So, can we be holy and host the Father? Yes.

In 1 Corinthians 6:18-20 Paul amplifies the meaning of cleansing the temple.

Flee sexual immorality. Every sin that a man does is outside the body, but he who commits sexual immorality sins against his own body. Or do you not know that **your body is the temple of the Holy Spirit** *who is in you, whom you have from God, and you are not your own? For you were bought at a price; therefore glorify (the Father) in your body and in your spirit, which are (our Father's).*

We are more than spirit. Our entire being must be clean.

Satan is totally opposed to that. He wants control of the temple. In 2 Thessalonians 2:3-4 Paul writes:

Let no one deceive you by any means; for that Day will not come unless the falling away comes first, and the man of sin is revealed, the son of perdition, who opposes and exalts himself above all that is called God or that is worshiped, so that he sits as God in the temple of God, showing himself that he is God.

Satan wants to sit in our personal temple, ruling as the god of our life.

Jesus, on the other hand, wants us to be a "house of prayer" rather than a "den of iniquity."

Jesus cast out demons and healed all who were oppressed, cleansing people's personal temples.

Acts 10:38 proclaims:

(The Father) anointed Jesus of Nazareth with the Holy Spirit and with power, who went about doing good and healing all who were oppressed by the devil, for (the Father) was with Him.

We do as Jesus did—because we know who we are, children of the Father and joint heirs with Christ. In the coming move of the Father's fire, we 50+ers are going to be instrumental in setting many people free.

Contemporary Christianity has sometimes forgotten, it seems, that we are in a spiritual battle with Satan, taking back what he stole. We claim mental health issues or a variety of the psychological diagnoses when it is often a spirit from Satan demonizing someone and holding them in bondage. But we have the authority to cast Satan out and to set the oppressed free. This authority is part of our Kingdom walk as sons and daughters of the Father.

Jesus, the Bread of Life, also demonstrated other desires from the Father when He cleansed the temple. God's people had forgotten the daily manna was the Father's provision for their lives. They instead created their own daily existence. Filthy mammon became their daily manna. They relied on money and profit, abandoning the reality and sanctity of the Father's dwelling place. It took the Living Bread to stand in stark contrast to false sustenance of money and oppression.

As time passes in a Christian's life it can become easy to take our eyes off the "Bread of Life" who is sustaining us. We can get into a routine and even rituals instead of living in daily relationship.

But we refuse to "go back to Egypt." We are part of a new and living way and will live in His faith.

Hebrews 10:19-25 puts it this way:

Therefore, brethren, having boldness to enter the Holiest by the blood of Jesus, by a new and living way which He consecrated for us, through the veil, that is, His flesh, and having a High Priest over the house of God, let us draw near with a true heart in full assurance of faith, having our hearts sprinkled from an evil conscience and our bodies washed with pure water. Let us hold fast the confession of our hope without wavering, for He who promised is faithful. And let us consider one another in order to stir up love and good works, not forsaking the assembling of ourselves together, as is the manner of some, but exhorting one another, and so much the more as you see the Day approaching.

We stay pure in our confession and love of the Father and we reach out in Kingdom love to others as well.

Together, we make up one glorious temple. Notice that each one of us is to be a temple piece. Each is individually created with the same substance or material. Then each of us is individually shaped to fit in the temple structure.

Ephesians 2:19-22 elaborates:

Now, therefore, you are no longer strangers and foreigners, but fellow citizens with the saints and members of the household of (the Father), having been built on the foundation of the apostles and prophets, Jesus Christ Himself being the chief cornerstone, in whom the whole building, being **fitted together**, *grows into a holy temple in the Lord, in whom you also are being built together for a dwelling place of (the Father) in the Spirit.*

We are not to live our lives separated and alone. We belong to a family. Sometimes family members have to help each other. Spiritually mature brothers and sisters can help you with the temple cleansing.

A few decades ago, during the height of the Charismatic Movement, "deliverance" became a recognized need for many believers. Questions arose about whether a believer could actually be demon possessed or demon oppressed. Books on deliverance were written and because of some extreme examples or because some people took the issue to an extreme, deliverance from demonic oppression seemed to die down. It seems we threw the baby out with the bathwater.

The church of Jesus Christ today is now recognizing that we have authority over demons and demonic oppression in Christian lives. We are not to fear these demonic spirits that can create havoc in a Christian's life and stop the person from living in true identity with the Father and with other Christians.

At MorningStar Ministries we have a "Freedom Team" that deals with demonic oppression in people's lives as well as with inner healing from past abuses and hurts. They are trained prayer warriors who help those who attend church live in freedom from demonic oppression and influence. Some major ministries also have a good track record for handling deliverance.[2]

We need each other's help in order to be whole. That's what family is all about.

When we are whole, we put on our spiritual armor because we live in the Spirit. We fight against the enemy to drive him out of our lives and usher in the Kingdom to those around us and even to nations.

Our identity is with the Father and His dear Son Jesus Christ. We have the Holy Spirit leading us into all truth. We rise up to take the Kingdom wherever our Father wants us to go.

We even help those who are spiritually orphaned to rediscover their family. That's what the next chapter is all about.

---

2. Ken Fish has had a remarkable healing and deliverance ministry in many countries of the world. His website is kingdomfireministries.org. You can find valuable resources there. Randy Clark has also done wonderful work in healing and deliverance ministry. You can find out more on his website: https://globalawakening.com. Derek Prince, Neal Anderson, and others also have excellent information and resources.

No Orphans Here

Let us do good to all, especially to those who are of the household of faith. (Gal 6:10)

O ne of the greatest ploys of our enemy, Satan, is his attempt to separate us from living in a Kingdom family relationship.

The MorningStar Ministries 50+ers have declared generational blessings to hundreds and hundreds of people who come to visit during conferences and at other times.[3] At the conclusion of these generational blessings, we always address the possible presence of the orphan spirit. We do this because so many Christians feel they are not connected to brothers and sisters in the body of Christ. Sometimes they have been hurt in the church. At times they may have felt rejected by a loved one or another Christian.

---

3. When we do generational blessings, we have a father and mother in the Lord to do the blessing when possible. They do not have to be husband and wife. Of course, you can do this by yourself also. We take a minute to explain blessings—for example, how the Father blessed Adam and Eve in Genesis 1:28, how patriarchs pronounced blessings, and how Jesus actually put out His hands and blessed His followers as He ascended to the Father (Luke 24:50-51). We tell them to keep their eyes open, and we look right in their eyes and allow the Holy Spirit to give us a short word of blessing—the power is in the brevity of the word that will touch their spirit. Then we seal the blessing.

After the generational blessing, which really declares something of power or purpose for their future lives, they are often deeply touched. But if they don't feel part of the family of God, the prophetic blessing they receive may not take root as it should.

So we call them back into the family of God with us, united in the body of Christ, never to feel as an outsider again. If we sense that an actual orphan spirit of the enemy has tormented them, lied to them, and separated them from the Kingdom family, we deal with it.

These precious people are part of the family of God, under the covering of their loving Father. We say to them we stand with them as fathers and mothers in the Lord and members of the body of Christ, all connected to each other, to Jesus, and to the Father. They will no longer feel like outsiders. We stand together in Kingdom life and purpose as sons and daughters of the Father. No orphans in this family.

Our Father has sons and daughters. All of us have been brought back to Him to live our lives in the family of God in His kingdom.

The orphan spirit from Satan attempts to separate us from each other, lessening the impact of Christ's body on earth. Anyone who has been wounded or abused in some way will be attacked by Satan, who wants to make the separation and hurt permanent and deep.

Church splits and Christians not going to church anymore can often be attributed to the demonic orphan spirit that wants to separate members of the body of Christ from each other.

Even the Apostle Paul had to address the issue of church "splits" and division. He wrote some powerful directions to the church groups in Galatia. He, a prominent Pharisee who had persecuted the church, was miraculously converted. He spent many years after that, growing in his new life in the Spirit, as he explains to the Galatian churches in his epistle. He had to give up his past beliefs and experiences to live the new life in the Spirit daily. He explains all this to the Galatian Christians and then boldly admonishes them:

> *O foolish Galatians! Who has bewitched you that you should not obey the truth, before whose eyes Jesus Christ was clearly portrayed among you as crucified? This only I want to learn from you: Did you receive the Spirit by the works of the law, or by the hearing of faith? Are you so foolish? Having begun in the Spirit, are you now being made perfect by the flesh?* (Gal 3:1-3)

The Galatians were returning to old beliefs and no longer walking in the unity of the Spirit. And why was this? It was because they were "bewitched." A spirit from Satan was breaking them up. Satan was in the camp, and they didn't even know it. After being freed from Satan's grasp and the religious rules they had followed, they were now returning to fleshly ways. In essence, they were once again becoming orphans, not linked with each other in the Spirit as the body of Christ.

We want to remove the orphan spirit forever.

I should know. I lived with the orphan spirit dominating my spiritual life for three decades until that pivotal moment when the Father hugged me.

When I was rejected (spiritually abused) by my spiritual parents who represented the church, the orphan spirit established a stronghold from my wound and set up camp.

After I was wounded, I felt like an outsider in church.

After my wife and I moved to Chicago many years later, a young man from California named Shawn Bolz, who people said operated in words of knowledge and prophetic gifts, visited a group of about 20 of us at a church in Chicago. He looked toward me and said he couldn't look directly at me but had to keep looking over my head. "You've been on the shelf for 30 years," he said. He was right.

But the morning God the Father came up behind me, put His arms around me, and hugged me, my life was transformed. The spiritual wound I had been carrying for more than 30 years was healed. The orphan spirit cannot be where Father God is.

Before the Father's hug, I had sought recognition from spiritual leaders at times. I just wanted to be affirmed. I didn't know the orphan spirit was attacking my heart. I remember coming to MorningStar Ministries in 2003 and trying to catch the eye of two speakers who were sitting at a table having lunch. (Won't someone please see me? Won't someone please recognize me?) Of course, they didn't see me. They were simply having lunch. I, on the other hand, was looking for a father to love this orphan.

When the Father hugged me, I no longer needed a spiritual authority to affirm me or recognize me, which I had desired for decades because of that spiritual wound.

I have found many Christians in their 50s and beyond who still do not have their identity grounded in the Father's love. My charismatic generation knew much about Jesus our Savior and about the Holy Spirit. We would confidently say we have a relationship with Jesus and that we are filled with the Holy Spirit. But I didn't hear many talk about their relationship with the Father. We seem to know a lot about the Father, whom we normally call God. But we don't necessarily identify with Him. We identify with His Son.

Of course we must identify with Jesus and have a relationship with Him. However, we sometimes may not focus on the reasons Jesus came to earth. One of the main reasons was to "glorify the Father," as John 17:1 says.

Jesus is our Lord and Savior. He is also our elder brother. But we can still feel like an orphan if we do not fully understand that Jesus' goal was to reveal the Father to us and place us in His family, as Luke 10:21-22 shows.

In that hour Jesus rejoiced in the Spirit and said, "I thank You, Father, Lord of heaven and earth, that You have hidden these things from the wise and prudent and revealed them to babes. Even so, Father, for so it seemed good in Your sight. All things have been delivered to Me by My Father, and **no one knows who the Son is except the Father, and who the Father is except the Son, and the one to whom the Son wills to reveal Him.** *"*

Immediately after Jesus' resurrection, He met Mary Magdalene by His tomb and called her name. She then recognized her risen Savior. Jesus then said to her,

Do not cling to Me, for I have not yet ascended to My Father; but go to My brethren and say to them, 'I am ascending to **My Father and your Father,** *and to My God and your God.'* (Jn 20:17)

The resurrected Jesus let His disciples know His Father was their Father. They would never be orphans.

The Gospels are filled with examples of Jesus revealing His Father and His Father's love. Jesus died for us to restore our relationship with the Father.

People's perceptions of the Father, however, may still be clouded by personal hurts from father figures or from spiritual wounds. In these cases they see the Father through their own imperfect lenses rather than through Jesus' perfect understanding. Satan will keep the distortion going as much as he can.

Very often these Christians need an inner healing. We 50+ers are called to heal their hurts. To know more about inner healing I highly recommend Christian Healing Ministries.[4]

---

4. Francis and Judith McNutt have headed this wonderful ministry for decades. Their volunteers

The Apostle Paul himself lived as a spiritual orphan until his remarkable encounter on the road to Damascus.

As Saul of Tarsus he knew the "traditions of the fathers" well before he had his heavenly encounter. He respected the fathers before him and followed what they said. He later told the Galatians,

"I advanced in Judaism beyond many of my contemporaries in my own nation, being more exceedingly zealous for the traditions of my fathers." (Gal. 1:14)

Those traditions led him to persecute the Christians with great zeal.

The problem with following the traditions of his fathers was that they were not looking to Father God. They were spiritual orphans who began creating their own religion and belief system, their own religious traditions, just as some of our own fathers have done through the centuries.

Saul of Tarsus was acting as an orphan, not understanding relationship, trying to please a God who controlled him. Paul the apostle discovered a new God, a relational God, a Father.

Although Saul of Tarsus had grown up in Jewish tradition, he as the Apostle Paul now knew the God of the New Testament, his Father. Paul had a relationship with the Father that transcended his Jewish traditions.

As I showed in Part One, Paul frequently opened his epistles with the salutation that included the recognition that the eternal God is our Father, such as in Romans 1:7:

Grace to you and peace from **God our Father** *and the Lord Jesus Christ.*

---

help those who come to Jacksonville, Florida, for healing. For more information about their ministry and for training materials, you can go to https://www.christianhealingmin.org

He recognized the Creator is our Father—personal and loving. God, the Creator of heaven and earth, is in relationship with us. His eternal purpose from the very beginning of creation was to have a loving relationship with sons and daughters.

In Romans 8:14-17 Paul amplifies the thought. I substituted the word *Father* for the word *God* at places in the passage to help us think in terms of the Eternal God being a personal Father:

> *For as many as are led by the Spirit of (our Father), these are sons of (the Father). For you did not receive the spirit of bondage again to fear, but you received the Spirit of adoption by whom* **we cry out, "Abba, Father."** *The Spirit Himself bears witness with our spirit that we are children of (the Father), and if children, then heirs—heirs of (the Father) and joint heirs with Christ, if indeed we suffer with Him, that we may also be glorified together.*

"Abba, Father" reveals Paul's understanding of the God of the New Testament. "Abba" is a term of endearment. It's like saying Papa. It shows warmth, love, and relationship. We are joined in a family.

"Father" is a title. It lets us understand our relational position as sons and daughters to a father. It carries with it the aspects of the position of a father: authority, control, decision maker, overseer, the leader, protector, supplier, higher in position and knowledge and experience than a son or daughter.

When you know your identity as the Father's son, you are not an orphan.

All of Romans 8 gives great insight into our Father's heart for us. It takes us from our earthly kingdom into His eternal Kingdom. It reveals the Father's plans.

That doesn't mean we have no issues when we know the Father. It means we will overcome, even death itself, because of the Father's love for us.

Romans 8:28-29 tells the destiny of those who love the Father:

And we know that all things work together for good to those who love (the Father), to those who are the called according to His purpose. For whom (the Father) foreknew, He also predestined to be conformed to the image of His Son, that He might be the firstborn among many brethren.

The Father had a plan for us even before we were born. We were to look like His Son. We were to be joint heirs with Him. Wow. This is our Father's plan for us.

It is very different from the plans those living in Christian culture make. Religion says you get your identity by what you do. The Father says you get your identity by who you are.

Romans 8:31-32 reveals how much the Father was willing to do for us as sons and daughters:

What then shall we say to these things? If (our Father) is for us, who can be against us? He who did not spare His own Son, but delivered Him up for us all, how shall He not with Him also freely give us all things?

Romans 8:38-39 explains our inseparable connection with Him:

For I am persuaded that neither death nor life, nor angels nor principalities nor powers, nor things present nor things to come, nor height nor depth, nor any other created thing, shall be able to separate us from the love of (our Father) which is in Christ Jesus our Lord.

The apostle now knew he was connected to a loving Father, and nothing could separate him from that relationship.

I counseled a woman from Europe who came to Morning-Star. She was trying to turn her country back to the Lord, she told me. She had worked for years battling religious strongholds in her country. She would have some success and make some significant connections, even in the government. Ultimately, however, she would be worn down.

She came to MorningStar to get healed up and to define new strategies. When we met in my office, she showed me the strategies the Lord had given her. She listed key people in her country who already knew what she was doing or who could help. She also listed those who were the religious figureheads in the country and who would try to stop any spiritual breakthrough from happening.

She had been in this battle for her country for years. She said it felt like she was in a repetitive cycle where she would make some headway, have some setbacks, and then become exhausted in the battle itself.

She told me she felt like an Esther who needed a Mordecai to cover her.

As soon as she said this, I thought, "Orphan." I immediately knew she didn't really know who she was. She was battling, trying to win the country for the Lord, but was lacking her real identity.

As a result she was acting like a worker for God, wanting to do all she could to win the nation for Him. But a key ingredient for success was missing from her life. She didn't understand the Father wanted a relationship with Her far more than He wanted her works for Him.

She interceded often for her nation. I asked her if she simply sat at times, meditating on the Father and His love. She responded that she prayed often to Him.

That wasn't the right answer. She didn't understand she was a daughter of a loving Heavenly Father, that she was of Royal heritage, that she had authority as His daughter to break down strongholds. Instead she had been trying to break down strongholds through her own plans and strategies. She acted as a spiritual orphan, not as a daughter.

During our time together we discussed the orphan spirit that had kept her from living in her true identity. We bound it and told it to leave her. Then we called for the Holy Spirit to heal and replace that broken area of her life and to have the Father's love fill her.

As part of my suggestions, I told her to go on some Father/daughter dates before she went back to her home country. Take some walks and see the beauty of the Father's creation. Talk to the Father, thanking Him for creating beauty, including having a beautiful daughter.

We have been born into a beautiful, eternal family. Our Father has created this earth and all its fullness for us. He also holds us together in loving relationship. Although Satan wants to make us as orphaned as he is, he can't when we recognize his schemes and cast him out of our lives.

Do you feel separated from the Father's love? Ask the Holy Spirit to reveal the reason. Our Father stands with you. He is concerned about you. Be strong and of good courage. He will help you and let you see that He never left you or forsook you. (Deut 31:5) Satan has used a hurt in your life to put a wedge between you and the Father and His church. You have authority to expel his lies.

In the great move of the Father that's coming, He is going to turn the eyes of His children back on Him. His fire is going to burn away the orphan spirit so we can live in a fiery identity as sons and daughters, bringing the Kingdom wherever we are, living in relationship with the family of God and doing exploits, no matter our age.

Walking In Anointing

But you have an anointing from the Holy One,
and you know all things. (1 Jn 2:20)

J esus knows who He is--the Son of the Father living from the Father's love in identity and purpose.

After Jesus spends 40 days in the wilderness, Satan tempts Him, wanting Him to reject His identity and purpose and instead have all the world's goods and adoration. Matthew 4:8-9 records,

> *The devil took Him up on an exceedingly high mountain, and showed Him all the kingdoms of the world and their glory. And he said to Him, "All these things I will give You if You will fall down and worship me."*

Because Jesus knows His identity, He can reject any temptation, even when He is at His weakest physical moments from 40 days of fasting. He rejects the fallen angel who now lives as a spiritual orphan in rebellion.

As for Jesus, He has an anointing from His Father, giving Him power to live in identity and purpose, glorifying the Father.

When Jesus is in Nazareth, He goes to the synagogue and reads the prophecy from the book of Isaiah, which starts, "The Spirit of the Lord is upon Me, Because He has anointed Me." (Luke 4:18) Then He declares to them, "Today this Scripture is fulfilled in your hearing." (Luke 4:21)

After Jesus' resurrection and ascension to the Father, Peter recalls how Jesus acted on earth, saying, "(The Father) anointed Jesus of Nazareth with the Holy Spirit and with power, who went about doing good and healing all who were oppressed by the devil, for (the Father) was with Him." (Acts 10:38)

From identity flows anointing.

I began to understand that from a personal experience I had on one of the saddest days of my life--Sunday, December 4, 2011.

I was sitting next to the middle aisle on the front row of our MorningStar Fellowship Church. My brother was on my right. My son Carson and his family were on the front row with me, too. Other relatives who came to be with me were there as well. I had asked the head usher if he could save some space for us because of all the relatives who were with me. I didn't realize until I got to church that they had reserved the front row.

I sat there in a griever's type of shock as the morning service progressed. That afternoon we were to have the memorial service for my wife of 43 years who had gone to heaven. The time from her death until this Sunday morning was a blur of sadness.

I didn't know then it would also be the beginning of an understanding of the Father's anointing.

That morning Wellington Boone, as guest speaker at MorningStar Fellowship Church, gave the morning message. His text was Isaiah 61. Wellington is an animated speaker and feels free to roam when he speaks. He had everyone open their Bibles to the passage as he stepped down from the platform. He stopped and stood directly beside me. He didn't know who I was or why I was sitting where I was sitting. He bent down, leaned over my shoulder, and read the first three verses of Isaiah 61 directly from my Bible slowly:

"The Spirit of the Lord God is upon Me,

Because the Lord has anointed Me

To preach good tidings to the poor;

He has sent Me to heal the brokenhearted,"

The words hit my broken heart as he read.

"To proclaim liberty to the captives,

And the opening of the prison to those who are bound;

To proclaim the acceptable year of the Lord,

And the day of vengeance of our God;

To comfort all who mourn,

To console those who mourn in Zion,

To give them beauty for ashes,

The oil of joy for mourning,

The garment of praise for the spirit of heaviness;

It was hard to stay sitting up in my seat. I was shaking and trying all I could to keep my composure as the words poured over me. My brother put his arm around me to steady me.

Then Wellington said the words that followed were for those people just mentioned.

That they may be called trees of righteousness,

The planting of the Lord, that He may be glorified."

Wellington continued his message. He walked in front of the rest of my relatives and talked about the second part of Isaiah 61, saying those who had been spoken about in the first three verses had a bright future. They were to be resource people the Lord was going to use.

This prophetic chapter proclaims that from the anointing flowing through Jesus those set free have bright futures.

The chapter continues:

And they shall rebuild the old ruins,
They shall raise up the former desolations,
And they shall repair the ruined cities,
The desolations of many generations.
Strangers shall stand and feed your flocks,
And the sons of the foreigner
Shall be your plowmen and your vinedressers.
But you shall be named the priests of the Lord,
They shall call you the servants of our God.
You shall eat the riches of the Gentiles,
And in their glory you shall boast.
Instead of your shame you shall have double honor,
And instead of confusion they shall rejoice in their portion.
Therefore in their land they shall possess double;
Everlasting joy shall be theirs.

As I write this, some years have passed. The Father has more than doubled my family. I have a new wife and three more sons to go with my son and daughter. I have nine grandchildren instead of four. I have been blessed with new life and direction.

The Father also placed an anointing on me and in me to call my 50+ generation to life, repairing what was broken and ruined.

He gave me a download on how I, and my generation, get to

do generational blessings, helping repair the desolation that can be found in the generations.

Although I had been in business and other ventures previously in my life, I became ordained as a pastor, one of the "priests of the Lord."

I truly feel I am walking in double blessing. I get to do these things. I get to minister to others as a son of the Father. I get to love unconditionally, without requiring some kind of return.

Wellington Boone had been used to give me a prophetic word on one of the saddest days of my life, and I am now living that word.

Over the years I have often reread the Isaiah 61 passage.

But I didn't realize until much later that the first verse of Isaiah 61 is the key to the entire passage. It begins, "The Spirit of the Lord God is upon Me, because the Lord has anointed Me...."

Let me put it my way. "The Spirit of the Father is upon Me, because the Father has anointed Me...."

All that Jesus did, as this prophetic chapter about the coming Messiah states, happened because the anointing from the Father was upon Him.

We carry that same anointing.

Some of us older charismatics may say something like, "I feel the Holy Spirit's anointing," We should remember that it was the Father's promise that the Holy Spirit would come. Before Jesus ascended to heaven, He told His disciples, "Behold, I send the Promise of My Father upon you; but tarry in the city of Jerusalem until you are endued with power from on high." (Luke 24:49)

The Father gives the anointing. This is as it should be. Sons and daughters receive the blessings from their Father.

I'm not trying to parse words. My point is that our Father

who cares for us so much blesses us with an anointing. We who have experienced so much of life, including the tragic and sad, receive an anointing that changes everything.

Let's review some of the aspects of the anointing the Father wants to place on us. It's the same anointing He placed on Jesus.

We get:

- To "preach good tidings to the poor," to those who are spiritually and physically in need of the Father's riches, offering them a way out.

- To "heal the brokenhearted." There are so many Christians and non-Christians who suffer from a broken heart.

- To "proclaim liberty to the captives," setting them free from sin, addictions, demonic inroads, and circumstances.

- To open "the prison doors to those who are bound" and trapped by the enemy of their souls. We have that anointing. Wow.

- To "proclaim the acceptable year of the Lord," letting others know the great news of the Kingdom.

- To proclaim "the day of vengeance of our God," not threatening them but warning them because we love them as the Father loves them and wants them to be spared.

- "To comfort all who mourn, to console those who mourn in Zion." We have a special anointing to wrap our arms around those who mourn, bringing them comfort and hope, letting them know that this, too, shall pass and we stand with them during the mourning.

- To give mourners "beauty for ashes, the oil of joy for mourning, the garment of praise for the spirit of heaviness." We have an anointing from the Father to turn mourners' sadness into resurrection life, so "that they may be called trees of righteousness, the planting of the Lord, that He may be glorified."

We do all this "that He (the Father) may be glorified." That anointing rests on us, is in us, and works through us, bringing glory to our loving Father, setting people free and establishing them as the Father's own plantings—trees of righteousness.

We, His sons and daughters, get to work in the Father's orchard, planting those who were formerly broken, bound up, imprisoned, destitute, grief stricken. They now become healthy and righteous members of the Father's family. And we are the ones who walk in the anointing, setting the captives free from their wounds of the past.

Then they (and we) get to walk out the rest of the prophetic words over them (and us) from Isaiah 61.

They and we:

- Shall "rebuild the old ruins" and "raise up the former desolations." What the enemy had tried to destroy and make of no value, we will turn around and make it like new. Lives that were nearly destroyed will be renovated and rebuilt in the Spirit.

- Shall "repair the ruined cities." This goes beyond families and into our culture. The anointing from the Father allows us to make things right and to re-establish righteousness where we live. We work in the harvest field.

- We will also repair "the desolations of many generations." We have the authority to break generational curses over our families and others in our community. No matter how long the desolation has existed and how desolate things look, we have an anointing from the Father to turn it around.

- Because we are royal heirs, others will take care of many of our needs--handling our "flocks," plowing our fields, cultivating our grape vines. We will be kings in the Father's house.

- We will also be "priests of the Lord," carrying a Melchizedek-type anointing as both kings and priests.

- They will recognize us as "servants of our God," or, to put it in 21-century vernacular, they shall recognize us as sons and daughters of an awesome Father.

- We will receive blessings from their hands. They will end up giving us glory because they recognize who we are and whom we represent. We will have "double honor."

- We will not have "confusion" or double-mindedness or lack of clarity because we know who we are. And "therefore in (our) land (we) shall possess double.

- And we end up with "everlasting joy."

Isaiah 61 continues. Verse 9 is especially wonderful:

Then their (our) offspring will be known among the nations,

And their (our) descendants in the midst of the peoples.

All who see them will recognize them

Because they are the offspring whom the Lord has blessed.

Our Father not only makes promises to us; He pays the blessing forward, covering our offspring as well.

The anointing of the Holy Spirit, directly from the Father, rests on us, His sons and daughters. That anointing carries spiritual authority and power.

As the fire of God our Father touches us, we are cleaned and purified. We then operate from His anointing. In our own strength we don't have the power to set the captives free and heal all those we touch. However, the spiritual power from the anointing that rests on us and is in us as His sons and daughters gives us that authority.

When we have an anointing, we get to distribute it to others. We don't pray, "Lord, if it's Your will, heal my mother." Instead we speak as Peter did, "Silver and gold I do not have, but what I do have I give you: In the name of Jesus Christ of Nazareth, rise up and walk." (Acts 3:6)

Through a time of prayer and fasting, ask for an anointing of the Father. Then expect Him to do things through you. Anticipate Him connecting you with some younger men or women who need the love of a father or mother in the Lord. Or, you might be like a Jonah whose very presence made a city repent.

You might even have an anointing to help bring in a righteous government. You can get with some other 50+ers to intercede for government. You can even be involved in local elections. If you are no longer working, you have more time to bring a Godly influence even into local elections.

If you have been in business, you can ask the Father to connect you to a younger entrepreneur or someone who needs a prayer covering in their work. Don't be surprised if the Lord gives you prophetic words for them or reveals some things for you to pray about that will bring breakthrough in their lives. You've been trained and now carry an anointing.

You carry an anointing that changes the very atmosphere. Some MorningStar 50+ers go on weekly prayer walks around nearby schools. They pray protection over the property and students. They pray for bullying to stop. They pray that the teachers will teach righteous principles. These 50+ers are unobtrusive, normally standing or walking on the sidewalk by the school property after school. They don't bring attention to themselves. They bring a Godly atmosphere to the property and those on it.

When I was growing up and going to our little Pentecostal church, we would often sing, "To be like Jesus, to be like Jesus.

All I ask, to be like Him." Through the years I understood that to mean we should live pure lives and be good Christians. I didn't realize it means much more. We have Christ in us. We carry an anointing to do what Jesus did and bring many more into the Kingdom and to bring a Kingdom culture to earth.

Honing Our Skills

Then he took his staff in his hand; and he chose for himself
five smooth stones from the brook, and put them in a
shepherd's bag, in a pouch which he had, and his sling was
in his hand. And he drew near to the Philistine.
(1 Sam 17:40)

Some years ago Tom Brokaw, a famous TV newscaster, wrote a book called *The Greatest Generation.* It told the story of those men and women who valiantly sacrificed themselves to protect our nation and the whole world from totalitarianism. They stood in the gap for our freedom when totalitarianism was sweeping Europe and the Pacific Rim with deadly force, including bombing Pearl Harbor.

These men came home, began families, and started the great economic boom in the post-World War 2 years. Their heroism made the United States the world's greatest power for peace and prosperity.

About 20 years after World War 2 ended, another conflict called up the next generation of young men. It was the Vietnam Conflict and became known as the first war we lost. The men who fought and returned home were spat upon and belittled.

These heroes were blamed for our political mistakes. Many of them have stayed separated from society. We still see some "Hell's Angels" type bikers, aging Vietnam vets traveling the nation's roads in their own, separated way. Most of us can tell stories of these vets who still remain among us and carry wounds from the war in their hearts, some still living drug-dependent lives.

During the first 50+ Gathering I led at MorningStar Ministries in 2013, we had an evening of open sharing, praying for healing from past wounds, whatever the wounds were. I was taken off guard when a 50+er confessed his guilt for escaping to Canada so he would not have to fight in Vietnam and has lived with remorse for that act ever since. Another man said he still carried guilt for not being qualified to enlist during that time. He wanted to defend his nation the way the "Greatest Generation" had. Another 50+er stood up and told how when her father returned from Vietnam, the family was destroyed because the war trauma he carried deeply wounded his wife and children.

Recently I was overseeing a 50+ worship night at our MorningStar Fellowship Church. We were singing Christmas carols, some of them made popular when we were children. We were relaxed in each other's company, sharing a common heritage and just being together without other generations present. It seemed we could be "family."

As we sang, we had freedom to be ourselves. During that evening, I sensed something very strange, however. Many of us carried a type of sadness deep within. It seemed to be part of our identity as a generation. We were not seen as winners. We were not like our parents who had ushered in times of prosperity and freedom. Ours was the generation where men and husbands in general became criticized and diminished in the media. We became the Homer Simpson generation, carrying a loser's identity. Some of us have forgotten that Christ gives us our true identity beyond what those think with whom we're closely connected.

It's amazing how things can change, even in the lifespan of one family.

A great example of this is seen in the story of David. He is the youngest and least of his brothers. It seems his father doesn't even consider him when Samuel the prophet comes, looking to anoint a son of Jesse as the future king. David is just a shepherd, a nobody.

David, the shepherd herder, learns some important truths, however, when he is still a nobody shepherd. While He tends the sheep in the wilderness, he also communes with God. He learns to worship Him with the harp.

David even practices the weaponry skills of the slingshot when he is on the hillsides. If he wasn't the youngest son, he could end up being in the army as one of the sling experts that armies used in those days. It later becomes very obvious he is that good.

David also demonstrates courage as a nobody shepherd who loves God. He defends the flock against lions and bears. It seems something very important happens in David's heart when he is a nobody, recognized by no one. He sees the God of Israel as his help and strength. Sometimes being the least and a nobody is the best body to be. You could be the least also.

The Father has a great plan for David's life, but if David doesn't develop a relationship with the Father first and hone skills the Father will use, he could end up just as King Saul before him ended up. This young man, however, has discovered His identity and source of trust.

David is in the wilderness worshipping the Lord, developing his skills on the harp. His sheep hear his voice as Jesus said the sheep hear His own voice. David's voice is probably the harp. He has a lot of time to practice playing the harp. He gets so good that others take notice. When Saul is distressed and needs comforting, his servants look for a skillful harp player. First Samuel 16:16-18 records the incident:

Let our master now command your servants, who are before you, to seek out a man who is a skillful player on the harp. And it shall be that he will play it with his hand when the distressing spirit from God is upon you, and you shall be well."

So Saul said to his servants, "Provide me now a man who can play well, and bring him to me."

Then one of the servants answered and said, "Look, I have seen a son of Jesse the Bethlehemite, who is skillful in playing, a mighty man of valor, a man of war, prudent in speech, and a handsome person; and the Lord is with him."

And 1 Samuel 16:22-23 shows the results:

Then Saul sent to Jesse, saying, "Please let David stand before me, for he has found favor in my sight." And so it was, whenever the spirit from God was upon Saul, that David would take a harp and play it with his hand. Then Saul would become refreshed and well, and the distressing spirit would depart from him.

This happens before David's victory over Goliath. His harpist skills get him into a relationship with Saul that will allow Saul to even trust him to represent Israel against Goliath. The servant who knows about David also said he is "a man of war." What could that mean? It means that this man either heard or saw firsthand that David developed a unique skill used in battle—slingshot expertise.

One day David's father Jessie sends him to see how his three oldest sons, who are serving in the Israeli army, are faring.

David arrives and sees an army living in fear of a Goliath. David asks, "What shall be done for the man who kills this Philistine and takes away the reproach from Israel? For who is this uncircumcised Philistine, that he should defy the armies of the living God?" (1 Sam 17:26)

David's oldest brothers can't believe what their youngest brother is saying. Eliab, the oldest, immediately gets angry with David and says, "Why did you come down here? And with whom have you left those few sheep in the wilderness? I know your pride and the insolence of your heart, for you have come down to see the battle." (1 Sam 17:28)

So, even within a family, from youngest to oldest, we can see a great contrast.

Eliab may have some reasons to lash out. Perhaps he is jealous of David who was anointed and actually played the harp at times for King Saul. Maybe Jessie showed some favoritism to the youngest of his eight sons. Just maybe David wasn't perfect and helped contribute to his oldest brother's opinion of how he acts.

David, however, is not put off. This shepherd boy knows his God. He brashly exclaims to his brothers and others who are afraid to face Goliath on the battle field, "The Lord, who delivered me from the paw of the lion and from the paw of the bear, He will deliver me from the hand of this Philistine." (1 Sam 17:37)

But he isn't really brash. He is speaking facts based on his relationship with a Father who grew him up in the wilderness, facing bears and lions, building his courage. He has also developed a devastating military skill, thanks to his wilderness times with the sheep.

Then he speaks to Goliath with a Godly confidence, not being deterred by the Philistine's great height or massive spear or boastful words.

David says to the Philistine,

You come to me with a sword, with a spear, and with a javelin. But I come to you in the name of the Lord of hosts, the God of the armies of Israel, whom you have defied. This day the Lord will deliver you into my hand, and I will strike you and take your head from you. And this day I will give the carcasses of the camp of the Philistines to the birds of the air and the wild beasts of the earth, that all the earth may know that there is a God in Israel. Then all this assembly shall know that the Lord does not save with sword and spear; for the battle is the Lord's, and He will give you into our hands. (1 Sam 17:45-47)

You know the result.

Through the years David walks in his prophetic purpose and the skills, aptitudes, abilities, giftings, and callings he developed in his earlier years. He stands out as a warrior and king. He holds to his identity as a chosen vessel of the Lord. Before every battle he talks to the Father to find out what to do. He grows in intimacy with the Father as he matures. He wants the Father to be glorified.

We older Christians also have learned some important lessons along the way. Some of the skills and vocations and connections we didn't consider of Kingdom significance in the previous decades are really preparations the Father will have us use in our later years as "kings and priests."

Romans 8:28 takes on added significance:

And we know that all things work together for good to those who love God, to those who are the called according to His purpose.

And we can better identify with 1 Corinthians 2:9-10:

But as it is written: "Eye has not seen, nor ear heard, nor have entered into the heart of man the things which God has prepared for those who love Him." But God has revealed them to us through His Spirit.

We are now ready to do greater things than at any time in our lives. We will bring the Kingdom to those around us and live in Godly peace.

When those of another generation or age now judge us, we can be the same as David if we have developed an identity as sons or daughters of the Father.

David's life was not easy. But he always ran to the source of His strength. The Psalms are filled with declarations of his trust in the Father, despite being attacked by enemies, being betrayed, and even having sinned.

Just one example of many that can be used from the Psalms is Psalm 56, where David says,

> *Be merciful to me, O God, for man would swallow me up;*
> *Fighting all day he oppresses me.*
> *My enemies would hound me all day,*
> *For there are many who fight against me, O Most High.*
> *Whenever I am afraid,*
> *I will trust in You.*
> *In God (I will praise His word),*
> *In God I have put my trust;*
> *I will not fear.*
> *What can flesh do to me?*

Towards the end of David's life, when he is a 50+er and has lived through the battles, the betrayals, the forgiveness from sins he had committed, and more, his focus is on the Father who helped and protected and forgave him.

Second Samuel 7:1-3 gives an amazing example of David's relationship with the Father.

> *Now it came to pass when the king was dwelling in his house,*
> *and the Lord had given him rest from all his enemies all*

around, the king said to Nathan the prophet, "See now, I dwell in a house of cedar, but the ark of God dwells inside tent curtains."

Then Nathan said to the king, "Go, do all that is in your heart, for the Lord is with you."

David simply wants to honor the Father by building Him a special place to dwell.

The Father tells Nathan what to say to David. One of the things the Father says in response is: "Also the Lord tells you He will make you a house."

Second Samuel 7:4-17 elaborates:

But it happened that night that the word of the Lord came to Nathan, saying, "Go and tell My servant David, 'Thus says the Lord: "Would you build a house for Me to dwell in? For I have not dwelt in a house since the time that I brought the children of Israel up from Egypt, even to this day, but have moved about in a tent and in a tabernacle. Wherever I have moved about with all the children of Israel, have I ever spoken a word to anyone from the tribes of Israel, whom I commanded to shepherd My people Israel, saying, 'Why have you not built Me a house of cedar?'"'

The Father seems overwhelmed by this spontaneous thought from His now mature son David:

Now therefore, thus shall you say to My servant David, "Thus says the Lord of hosts: 'I took you from the sheepfold, from following the sheep, to be ruler over My people, over Israel. And I have been with you wherever you have gone, and have cut off all your enemies from before you, and have made you a great name, like the name of the great men who are on the earth. Moreover I will appoint a place for My people Israel, and will plant them, that they may dwell in a place of their own and move no more; nor shall the sons of wickedness oppress them anymore, as previously, since the time that I commanded judges to be over My people Israel, and have caused you to rest from all your enemies. Also the Lord tells you that He will make you a house.

" 'When your days are fulfilled and you rest with your fathers, I will set up your seed after you, who will come from your body, and I will establish his kingdom. He shall build a house for My name, and I will establish the throne of his kingdom forever. I will be his Father, and he shall be My son. If he commits iniquity, I will chasten him with the rod of men and with the blows of the sons of men. But My mercy shall not depart from him, as I took it from Saul, whom I removed from before you. And your house and your kingdom shall be established forever before you. Your throne shall be established forever.' "

The Father promises a great blessing to David because David wants to glorify the Father:

According to all these words and according to all this vision, so Nathan spoke to David.

David is overwhelmed by his Father's love. Second Samuel 7:18-22 says:

Then King David went in and sat before the Lord; and he said: "Who am I, O Lord God? And what is my house, that You have brought me this far? And yet this was a small thing in Your sight, O Lord God; and You have also spoken of Your servant's house for a great while to come. Is this the manner of man, O Lord God? Now what more can David say to You? For You, Lord God, know Your servant. For Your word's sake, and according to Your own heart, You have done all these great things, to make Your servant know them. Therefore You are great, O Lord God. For there is none like You, nor is there any God besides You, according to all that we have heard with our ears.

David walked through many difficult circumstances in his life. So have 50+ers today. Even David's own brothers criticized him. Many 50+ers who found the Lord years ago have also been criticized. David made mistakes and sinned. So have we. David had to fight to save his family and his very own life at times. And it seems we 50+ers have had to do the same thing while trusting our Heavenly Father.

In all these circumstances we can come out like David did with promises from the Father for our children and our children's children. It may be difficult at times to keep our eyes fixed on the Father's plan when we feel marginalized. It has been difficult for many saints through the centuries. However, we have a more certain hope than anyone in the world. When society or organized religion or relatives speak lies to us and our generation, we consider the source and instead listen to the Father's loving voice for our future.

Romans 8:11 says:

*But if the Spirit of (the Father) who raised Jesus from the dead dwells in you, (**The Father**), who raised Christ from the dead,* **will also give life to your mortal bodies** *through His Spirit who dwells in you.*

The Father gives us life. He is the one who directed our paths and helped us learn and implement so many skills and ideas. It is He who created us. It is He who made our spiritual DNA and wants us to live fully in how He has uniquely and individually equipped us. He will give us life and energy to walk in our purpose that He has planned for us for more years than we can count.

- Are you weary?
- Are you spiritually exhausted?

- Are you frustrated that you still don't see the answers to your prayers you want to see?

- Are you uneasy because you are trying to figure out the Lord's will for your life?

Perhaps it's time to put first things first and rest from your own laboring.

"There remains therefore a rest for the people of God (that is, the children of our Heavenly Father). For he who has entered His rest has himself also ceased from his works as God (our Father) did from His." (Heb 4:9-10)

Give up the works and rest in the Father's love.

So, who are you?

You are a son/daughter of the Father. Period.

Holy heat will yet flow through you, and Godly glowing will rest on you. Tongues of fire will return. The Father has called you for such a time as this.

David was a nobody, a shepherd boy on the backside of the desert. Yet he was called to do great things. We have lived our lives to yet do great things also. We may not have had the success that David had, but we are not finished.

I believe the Father is moving especially on the "nameless, faceless" ones—those who are not seeking recognition but have their hearts fixed on the Father's love. A few years ago some "nameless, faceless" people in Dalton, Georgia, got together to pray. They cleaned out a storage room at the back of a gift shop owned by a Christian to make it a prayer room. Every Tuesday morning they met for prayer.

One Tuesday as they were praying, they noticed something coming down the edges of the wall. The next week when they prayed, more of this liquid came down the wall. For two years this happened. They realized it was a type of oil.

Then one of the 50+ men who had his Bible opened to a chapter in the Psalms saw liquid on the chapter and thought a grandchild had spilled something on a page in his Bible. But he quickly realized that this was oil. The oil kept spreading and covered all the pages of the Old Testament and then covered all the pages of the New Testament. He put the Bible in a plastic bag, and the bag started filling with this same oil. That was the beginning of a "wonder" of the Father, who operates in miracles, signs, and wonders. Since then many people from all over the world have come to Dalton every Tuesday morning to worship and be prayed for. Many are healed. Our God is bigger than the religious boxes we have tried to put Him in.

My point in this example is that these weekly prayer warriors are not famous pastors or evangelists. They are simply humble fire starters. They all have different spiritual backgrounds and different walks in their personal lives, but they have joined to pray for others and to intercede. God has shown up in a powerful way. He will be showing up in your life too in greater ways in the days ahead as you walk humbly before him.

He will give you the desires of your heart when your heart is aligned with the Father,

He is taking all the training and experiences from your earlier years and will now maximize your skills, aptitudes, abilities, giftings, and callings. He is making all things work together for good. Training is over. Now the Father is going to use all your past, which has now matured, so that it can be applied to situations and families and surroundings. We get to do things we never thought possible. And it won't be work!

Kingdom Generations

"You are My Son, Today I have begotten You.
Ask of Me, and I will give You the nations for Your
inheritance,
And the ends of the earth for Your possession." (Ps 2:7-8)

Fathers and mothers have sons and daughters, creating the generations. The timeline in the Old Testament is recorded by generations, not by years, and illuminates the importance of intergenerational connection.

The Old Testament works through the genetic generations. Our Father's autobiography traces our lineage all the way back to His first son and daughter, Adam and Eve. The family tree is extensive. Abraham has Isaac, Isaac has Jacob, Jacob (Israel) is the father of the 12 tribes, and so forth.

Spiritual intergenerational connections are also important in our Father's book. They include Elisha as a spiritual son of Elijah and Timothy as a spiritual son of the Apostle Paul.

The importance of generational relationship cannot be overstated. Elders sat in the gates of the cities in Israel as judges. Christ's very death and resurrection was to restore sons and daughters to the Father.

I have always used Joshua and Caleb as prime examples for what 50+ers get to do in their mature years. They lived faithfully, even through the 40 years in the wilderness, and then led the next generation into the Promised Land, a prophetic picture of what fathers and mothers in the Lord are also called to do today.

Although we might be intimidated by the thought we ourselves are to father or lead an entire generation or nation, the Father knows best for each of us. He has prepared each of us to connect all parts of the Kingdom.

The Bible gives us some great intergenerational examples of the older generation making a profound impact, even if it is with just one other person. Ironically perhaps, two books of the Bible that reveal a pair of these awesome older adults are named after the person in the next generation each is called to help. The books of Esther and Ruth demonstrate great intergenerational connection based on relationship.

The book of Esther is the story of a queen who only gets to be who she is because a mature older person in her life guides her path. The older person is Mordecai. Esther 2:7 records that when Esther's father and mother die, Mordecai steps in and "took her as his own daughter." Here is a man with a tender heart who wants to protect a close relative.

Life is not easy for the Jewish people at the time, living in subjection to a foreign nation and having to obey foreign laws. However, Mordecai stays true to his faith and guides Esther in the Jewish faith also as he watches her and helps her grow. He understands the purposes of God and communicates them to Esther.

Esther is a beautiful young woman and is chosen as one of those with potential to become the wife of King Ahasuerus. She is taken to the king's palace, along with other young beauties, and for a year is prepared to be as beautiful as possible in order to please the king and to perhaps become the next queen.

Every day Mordecai "paced in front of the court of the women's quarters," worrying about Esther's welfare and wondering what is happening to her, according to Esther 2:11. He is concerned about her welfare, even when it seems he is powerless to do anything about it.

Our Father is also calling mature men today to carry a heart for the next generation, even when it seems we have no control.

When Esther is presented before the king, she obtains favor and grace, and the king falls in love with her. I wonder how much of Mordecai's tender love toward his adopted daughter formed her character so wonderfully she actually shines more brightly than any other woman there.

King Ahasuerus crowns Esther queen, and Mordecai watches all this from the sidelines. Esther 2:20 says Esther did not reveal who her family was or that she was a Jew, "just as Mordecai had charged her, for Esther obeyed the command of Mordecai as when she was brought up by him." Even when Esther is queen, she respects her adopted father so much she will do what he thinks best. This doesn't sound like a man who bosses a child around.

This sounds to me like a man

- who knows how to love and give of himself,
- a man whose actions create trust,
- a man who thinks only the best for the child he is helping grow into a beautiful woman.

Mordecai is a real man, a mature man—and has a tender heart.

One day Mordecai, who is a watchman at the gate, hears there is a plot to kill the king, and he tells Queen Esther. The conspirators are captured and hanged, and Mordecai's name is written in the king's official journal. Mordecai could have kept quiet. After all, someone might find out he is Jewish and the adopted father of Esther. The Jews were not highly regarded. But he acts out of the integrity of his heart and saves the king.

I don't have to recount the entire book of Esther in order to demonstrate Mordecai's powerful influence. We are all familiar with how Haman, the king's second in command, wants to kill Mordecai and all Jews because as a Jew Mordecai refuses to go against his own faith and bow to Haman. Godly men today also have to live their faith.

Things go from bad to worse. Only a miracle can save Mordecai, Esther, and the rest of the Jews. Mordecai becomes a dramatic part of how the miracle unfolds. He acts wisely and with a heart that burns within him when he tells Esther what is happening and that she must intervene. This Godly man says to Esther, "If you remain completely silent at this time, relief and deliverance will arise for the Jews from another place, but you and your father's house will perish. Yet who knows whether you have come to the kingdom for such a time as this?" (Est 4:14)

Prophetic wisdom flows from Mordecai. And prophetic wisdom will flow from today's fathers in the Lord whose hearts are after the Father.

It may seem like we've labored for years, praying and worrying about our children or others under our authority. But we are not in the battle by ourselves. We are submitted to the direction of our Heavenly Father who wants the best for us and our families and is working all things together for good for us who love Him, as Romans 8:28 says.

Esther obeys Mordecai's directions to speak to the king, and Mordecai prays and fasts for three days, eating and drinking nothing. It is a life or death moment. There are times, too, in our own lives when life or death moments occur. How we respond determines the outcome. Mordecai, as part of the miracle, surrenders everything to God, trusting Him for the outcome.

And, what do you know, just as good Bible stories should, the miracle comes. While Mordecai is praying and fasting, King Ahasuerus has a restless night and has servants read the king's journal. And, sure enough, he is reminded that Mordecai had once saved his life.

Let's see here, a praying 50+er reaches the throne room of heaven, which makes a king wake up and just coincidentally read about him. To me that is the climax of the story. The rest is the dénouement, just the outcome. Wicked Haman is found out and is hanged on the gallows meant for Mordecai, Esther remains the queen, the Jews get revenge instead of being slaughtered, and Mordecai becomes second in command to the king.

Wow.

- A man with a heart of compassion takes a child in and treats her as his daughter for years.
- He shows her love and raises her in the faith.
- He worries about her welfare when she is no longer under his roof.
- He gives her Godly wisdom and some tough prophetic words.
- He prays and fasts for the right outcome to life's biggest problem.
- And the miraculous happens.

This 50+ man prophetically symbolizes we men are not finished. As we humble ourselves and pray, seeking miraculous answers during some very dark times, our Father who sees in secret will reward us openly. We, like Mordecai, are being called to cover a younger generation. We, like Mordecai, can also expect a miraculous outcome.

Now let's examine how this same principle works for Godly women. The second intergenerational example comes from the book of Ruth.

I have heard many sermons about Ruth. She is admired for her faithfulness, for her virtue, for her servant's heart. And, amazingly, she becomes the great grandmother of David.

However, I haven't heard any sermons about Naomi, the extraordinary mother in the faith who made all this possible. The book of Ruth chronicles Naomi's life story, and those of us who have walked through serious troubles can relate to many of her circumstances.

Naomi had everything when she was young. She lived in Bethlehem with a good husband, two sons, recognition in the community, and even wealth. Remember when we were young and in love? It seemed we had all of life's good fortunes ahead of us.

Then circumstances work against Naomi. She and her family have to leave Bethlehem and go to a foreign country because of a famine. How many of us have had circumstances in our lives that seemed to work against us, even as Christians, and we had to make decisions to keep things going. At the time we probably didn't realize this was our Father's hand, preparing us for something special in our later years.

When Naomi is in the foreign country of Moab, her husband dies. Many of us, too, have experienced death and loss. Some of us who were married or divorced stay single the rest of our lives, wanting to put the grief or hurts behind us, continuing to live, hoping for more.

Naomi still has two sons, however. And she can have some consolation that she is their mother.

She probably has mixed feelings when her sons marry women who are not from Judah. But it seems Naomi's heart is big enough to accept these daughters-in-law, even if it isn't what she thinks is the perfect plan. How many of us also have to love, even when things aren't the way we want them to be?

Then after another ten years pass, more tragedy strikes Naomi.

Her two sons die also. What can Naomi do? Her only recourse is to return to Bethlehem in the land of Judah because she hears the famine is over. Sometimes when it rains, it pours. Many of us 50+ers have to make decisions, seemingly out of desperation. We don't fully realize at the time that the Father has us under His wing of provision.

Despite Naomi's misfortunes it is obvious she has established a good relationship with her daughters-in-law. Before she returns to her homeland, she blesses them and kisses them and then releases them to stay in their home country.

Many of us 50+ers have also had to bless others and not curse our circumstance or our loss. Many of us have had to walk through the valley of the shadow of death and even give up those who are dear to us, even as Naomi did.

Living a Kingdom life isn't all blessings and prosperity. Living a Kingdom life strengthens us to overcome life's circumstances.

It must have been a real consolation to Naomi when her daughter-in-law Ruth decides to stay with her rather than in the safety and familiarity of her own country.

Ruth says, "Wherever you go, I will go; and wherever you lodge, I will lodge; Your people shall be my people, and your God, my God. Where you die, I will die, and there will I be buried." (Ruth 1:16)

Naomi has suffered many losses, but there is something about her and her God that makes Ruth cling to her. Naomi must have sensed life isn't all bad. There are some blessings along the way. For many of us who are older there also are times when we have to cling to a glimmer of hope when disappointments hit us.

When Naomi gets back to Bethlehem, her friends and relatives whom she hasn't seen in decades greet her with excitement. That must have felt strange to this woman who has suffered so much. Life has taken its toll on her. She says, "Don't call me Naomi," which means *pleasant*. "Call me Mara (which means *bitter*), for the Almighty has dealt very bitterly with me." Some of us today might be feeling the same thing. We are run over by life's twists and turns, even when we want to do the right things. It can be easy to look at circumstances and declare defeat or discouragement.

But in all of life's circumstances, something has happened to Naomi that she didn't realize. She has gained wisdom and insight that the Father would use for her ultimate blessing. How many of us may be in situations where we can't see the forest for the trees and can't view from the Father's perspective? But the Father understands all that and doesn't condemn us. He is working out all things for our and His good.

Ruth wants to help get provision for the two of them and asks her mother-in-law for permission to glean heads of grain in the field of a man named Boaz, one of Naomi's relatives.

Naomi says, "Go, my daughter." It is obvious that along the way, despite all the tragedies and shifts in life, Naomi has built a loving relationship with Ruth.

Naomi's personal love for her is so strong Ruth will do anything for her.

Boaz realizes Ruth's great love and respect for her mother-in-law and gives her favor to gather even more grain than would normally be the case.

It might be that sometimes we older adults don't see that, despite the circumstances that are against us, we are a powerful example to others, just as Naomi is to Ruth. Although Naomi calls herself *Mara*, that's not what Ruth would ever call the mother she loves.

Ruth comes back from gathering grain and reports all that has happened in the field and how Boaz has treated her with such kindness. Naomi now acts as a mature, wise mother in the faith, advising Ruth on what to do.

We 50+ers who have walked through so much have gained wisdom from the Father as we kept trusting Him.

Ruth obeys and continues to glean only in Boaz's fields until the end of the harvest.

As the third chapter of the book of Ruth begins, we see Naomi now speaking as a spiritual mother to Ruth. She says, "My daughter, shall I not seek security for you, that it may be well with you?" Then she instructs Ruth to dress in her finest clothes, go to the threshing floor where Boaz is winnowing barley that night, and lie at the feet of Boaz after he falls asleep.

Boaz wakes up in the middle of the night and discovers Ruth at his feet. He covers her up and tells her how he has watched her and how he respects her faithfulness to Naomi and recognizes her virtue and moral character.

Despite all the sad things that have happened in Naomi's life, she still has fostered a beautiful attractiveness in Ruth's life, including being virtuous. Sometimes we parents and grandparents may be surprised at what others see in our children. The Father has a way of working all things for our good.

Ruth returns to Naomi with a gift of grain from Boaz, and Naomi knows that Boaz is now going to do what he can to have Ruth become his bride. He redeems the land and also then has the freedom to marry Ruth.

That's a good story, but it is not the fairy-tale ending where Ruth and Boaz live happily ever after. There's even more.

Boaz and Ruth have a son.

Naomi's friends recognize the significance of that birth, saying to Naomi, "Blessed be the Lord, who has not left you this day without a close relative; and may his name be famous in Israel! And may he be to you a restorer of life and a nourisher of your old age." (Ruth 4:14-15)

And so it happens.

CARRYING THE FATHER'S FIRE

Naomi, who had borne so many trials throughout her life, holds the baby in her arms and becomes the child's nurse.

And Ruth 4:17 records:

*"The neighbor women gave him a name, saying, **There is a son born to Naomi**.' And they called his name Obed. He is the father of Jesse, the father of David."*

Can it be we 50+ers will be surprised at the gifts of life the Father has yet to bestow upon us, even in our very mature years? The fire of God that has purified our lives will change our vision and how we see around us.

We may cradle a grandchild who will one day do great things. Perhaps we will love a neighbor's child and win another Billy Graham to the Lord. Maybe we will even hold a nation's destiny in our hands, just as Naomi got to do.

You might want to consider sitting in a children's class at church, just to be a grandparent in the Lord. Don't be surprised if some of the younger ones want to sit on your lap. You can impart the Father's love to them just by being in the room with them.

The MorningStar 50+ers have become "heavenly hosts" in our church. We adopt students from MorningStar University. We pray over them and write them monthly, perhaps giving them a prophetic word or a $10 gift card to Chick-Fil-A. Some heavenly hosts take their student to lunch and meet with them every once in a while. Some of those students attribute their success to the covering of heavenly hosts while at MorningStar University. You can do the same thing where you are. Adopt a student or a younger couple or younger family. You will change their lives!

You can also be an active part of a small group in your church. Or, begin your own small group. Use what the Father has revealed to you in this book to bring them into identity and wholeness in the Father's love. Then look outward to make a difference by starting fires in others' lives.

As we live a Kingdom life over the decades, persuaded of our Father's heart and faithfulness, profound results follow.

Only the Father knows the end from the beginning. But we are assured our end will be worth every price we have had to pay. I think Mordecai and Naomi would say the same thing.

Conclusion

Everyone's going through a refining fire sooner or later, but you'll be well-preserved, protected from the eternal flames. Be preservatives yourselves. Preserve the peace.
(Mark 9:49-50, The Message)

During my 70 plus years on earth I have seen many moves of God. Growing up in a Pentecostal church helped. We were not afraid of the Holy Spirit's leading in our lives and church services. We would have testimonies at every Sunday night service, telling of something God worked out in a person's circumstances; some testimonies were fresh while some others were distant memories.

When I was about five years old, one of the great healing evangelists came to our town, Wausau, Wisconsin, and set up a tent across from Marathon Park, where the county fair was held each year. I remember being in that big, packed, white tent with all the other people, although I don't remember the message. What I do remember, though, is that the evangelist called people forward for prayer. My father didn't go forward but sent my older brother David and me up front.

We stood in a line across the front by the platform as the healing evangelist prayed for each person. It didn't take much when he prayed for me. Instantly I was on the ground. Next to me was my brother. What happened? He didn't push us. We fell under the power of the Holy Spirit. My parents smiled.

When my father was suffering from cancer in 1956, my mother requested a prayer cloth from Oral Roberts. It didn't come in time to place on my father, but my mother kept it to help her walk through her grief.

There have been many "moves of God" over the centuries and even in my lifetime. Each seems unique, even though common threads of God's power and purpose run through them all.

The Charismatic Movement swept in during the '60s and '70s, a move of the Holy Spirit through many denominations and across many nations that has continued.

The "faith" movement emerged. Deliverance ministry is now moving in authority. Major prophetic voices are now active.

It seems we see aspects of our Father's personality at different times, just as He revealed portions of Himself as *El Shaddai* (the all sufficient one) or *Jehovah-Jireh* (my provider) to Abraham and others long ago.

But something is changing. He is putting His full character on display. His fire is coming as the Great Harvest of the ages takes place. It will take every part of what He has shown through the ages to bring it in. We now are going to do the works of Jesus, not just read about them.

Jesus gave His disciples their marching orders, saying that wherever they went they were to proclaim, "The kingdom of heaven is at hand." Then He told them, "Heal the sick, cleanse the lepers, raise the dead, cast out demons. Freely you have received, freely give." (Matt 10:7-8)

These are our marching orders, too.

We now get to choose our future. When my wife of 43 years went to heaven, I could have chosen to live in grief and loss. Instead I chose the Father. Every morning I got up and made a declaration that I had taped on my bathroom mirror.

It said,

> I am part of the ecclesia, the governing body of the Lord. I govern in the Kingdom under the Father's authority.
>
> Father, I am ready for today's marching orders and will bring the Kingdom.
>
> I contend for the miracles I read in the Word.
>
> I call forth words of knowledge. I call forth healing.
>
> My eyes are holy unto the Lord. I see spiritually.
>
> I carry the atmosphere of the Lord and see many lives changed.
>
> I declare nations coming into the Kingdom.

Then I went to the living room in my home, raised my hands, and said, "I love you, Father. I love you, Father."

The declaration and worship made all the difference in my life and future. I did not know what my future would look like going forward, but the Father did, and I trusted Him.

Now the Father has blessed me with Sandy, a precious wife. We live to do the Father's will together.

The Father has revealed Himself to us. We have matured to see, accept, and understand His character, purpose, and power. We choose His future.

We know our time has come for the great next thing in our lives and in His Kingdom. Our Father has had it planned from the beginning as Psalm 139:16-17 says,

Your eyes saw my substance, being yet unformed.
And in Your book they all were written,

The days fashioned for me,

When as yet there were none of them.

How precious also are Your thoughts to me, O God!

How great is the sum of them!

So, we all now also get to declare the future He has prophesied, saying,

The fire of God is coming!

And we will carry it.

It will cleanse our minds, burning away past sins and failures from remembrance.

The old has passed from our lives. The new has come.

It will change our vision and how we see around us.

We have eyes to see the Father's Kingdom purpose.

Holy heat will flow through people, and Godly glowing will be on individuals. Tongues of fire will return.

We call His anointing fire into and over our lives to usher in the Kingdom.

This will be a new day, a day of the Lord, the time of the Great Harvest. It will be like the Great Awakening from the past but will be unlike any we have heard about. It will be unique and different.

We take our place, loved children of our Heavenly Father. We are cleansed and set free to start Godly fires and host the Great Harvest. Those around us will be changed. People and nations will be changed. The fires will become a blaze of glory.

We were born for this.

Also read John's amazing book, *50+: The Emerging Joshua and Caleb Generation.*

The book is designed to help you--

• **Know your calling and purpose as a 50+er.** We've been through a lot and have overcome. Now we will step into to the future that God has planned for us.

• **Discover how to bless other generations.** You will understand the importance of blessings, and you will have practical guidelines for you and other 50+ers to use. The 50+ers at MorningStar Ministries have blessed thousands of visitors and conference attendees coming to MorningStar, using these clear guidelines.

• **Create a spiritual legacy for your family and future generations.** This section of the book is also helpful if you want to meet with other 50+ers to create spiritual legacies.

Available on Amazon.com in both print and Kindle versions. Simply enter the following in the Amazon.com search field: *50+: the Emerging Joshua and Caleb Generation.*

MorningStar

See powerful sessions from previous MorningStar 50+ Gatherings.

Are you interested in learning more about inner healing or deliverance? Would you like to watch other sessions designed specifically for 50+ers? See 50+ Gathering sessions and sessions from other MorningStar conferences by subscribing to MorningStar TV.

Go to: **www.morningstartv.com** to learn about all the benefits of being a MorningStar TV subscriber.

Made in the USA
Columbia, SC
03 February 2020